gaz regan's

101 Best New Cocktails

VOLUME V

gaz regan's

101
Best
New
Cocktails

VOLUME V

gaz regan

mixellany limited

Copyright © 2016 Gary Regan

All rights reserved. Printed in the United Kingdom. No part of this book may be used or reproduced in any manner whatsoever without written permission except in the case of brief quotations embodied in critical articles and reviews. For information address: Mixellany Limited, 3 Eyford Cottages, Upper Slaughter, Cheltenham, Gloucestershire GL54 2JL United Kingdom or email mixellanyltd@googlemail.com.

Mixellany books may be purchased for educational, business, or sales promotional use. For information, please write to Mixellany Limited, 3 Eyford Cottages, Upper Slaughter, Cheltenham, Gloucestershire GL54 2JL United Kingdom. or email mixellanyltd@googlemail.com

First edition

ISBN 13: 978-1-907434-43-3

British Library Cataloguing in Publication Data.

A catalogue record for this book is available from the British Library

This book is dedicated to Global Bartending community.
You keep me young, guys. Ta Muchly!

ACKNOWLEDGEMENTS

As always, thanks go to all the bartenders who submitted recipes for this volume., and to Martha Schueneman, my trusty editor and sidekick.

Thanks, also, to Martin Doudoroff, for turning this book into an app, and to Jared Brown and Anistatia Miller who, for many years, have been turning my words into books!

gaz regan's 101 BEST NEW COCKTAILS VOLUME V

Contents

1831 by Tim Laferla, Red Bar @ Bam-Bou, London, UK	17
Alcatraz by Christin Wagner, La Petite Grocery, New Orleans, LA, USA	18
Ambré Carré by Agostino Galli, Lacerba, Milano, Italy	20
An Offer He Couldn't Refuse by Jason Simplot, Suite 410, Seattle, WA, USA	22
Angel's Share by Marcus Henriksson, Brooms & Hatches, Oslo, Norway	24
Apple of My IPA by Dustin Adams, The Cellar, Fullerton, CA, USA	27
Backyard Barbecue by Paulina Swan, ROUX, Rochester, NY, USA	29
BB King by Julian Serna, The Lo & Behold Group, Singapore	31
Bebe Lyon by Mary White, Palmer & Co., Sydney, NSW, Australia	33
Bee Negroni by Maxime Verrier, HIMKOK, Oslo, Norway	36
Black Ruby by Serena Bass, Lido, New York, NY, USA	38
Blind Spot by Danny Whelan, Kelvingrove Café, Glasgow, Scotland, UK	40
Bogmyrtle Blazer by Jesper Strauss, Le Mouton Noir + Tall Guy Spirits, Copenhagen, Denmark	42

Bonfire Banger by Benji Ryde, RYND Bar & Kitchen,
    Reading, Berkshire, UK   44

Bramble On by Anthony DeSerio and Ryan Henry
    Tunnacliffe, Sticks and Stones, Uncasville, CT, USA   46

Britoni by Antonio Anzelmo, Smith & Wollensky,
    London, UK   49

Burnt Brandy & Peach by Jon Yeager, PourTaste,
    Nashville, TN, USA   51

Charlie Wallbanger by Brian Nixon, McClellan's
    Retreat, Washington, DC, USA   53

Chartreuse Cobbler by Oron Lerner, French 57,
    Tel Aviv, Israel   55

Colleen Bawn Knickebein, Frederic Yarm, Loyal Nine,
    Cambridge, MA, USA   57

Devil's Pitchfork by Ted Kilgore, Planter's House,
    Saint Louis, MO, USA   60

Do-Right by Jared Fischer, Clement in the Peninsula
    Hotel, New York, NY, USA   62

Dom's Bomb, Ankit Dabral, Conservatory,
    Melbourne, Australia   64

Dye House by Samuel Nelis, Waterworks Food + Drink,
    Winooski, Vermont, USA   67

Early Evening Fizz by Nick Caputo, Sovereign Loss,
    London, UK   69

El Diablo Loco by Giuseppe Serra, The Palomar
    Restaurant, London, England, UK   71

Élysée Treaty by Ivan Mandaric, Oxbo Urban Bar & Grill, DoubleTree by Hilton Hotel, Zagreb, Croatia	74
Final Straw by Geoff Fewell, Boilermaker House, Melbourne, Victoria,	76
Five Finger Death Punch by David Adams, The Dead Canary, Cardiff, Glamorgan, UK	78
Forged & Bound by Jacques Bezuidenhout, Forgery, San Francisco, CA, USA	81
French Old-Fashioned, Pete Volkmar, Gourmet Galley Catering, North Stonington, CT, USA	83
Freshmaker by Eric Grenier, Honor Kitchen & Cocktails, Oakland, CA, USA	85
Full Blood by Michael Gatlin, Evo, Portland, Maine, USA	87
Garrigue by Karim Mehdi, SABA, Dublin, Ireland	89
Geraldine's Ginger Fizz by Chris Edwardes, Hidden House, Stari Grad, Croatia	91
Gilbert by Dushan Zaric, The 86 Co, New York, NY	93
Global Jukebox by Paul Zuber, Bank & Bourbon, Philadelphia, PA, USA	95
Golden Girls by Yi Chen, Berlyn Restaurant, Brooklyn, NY, USA	98
Golden Rose by Anthony Le, O Bar and Dining, Sydney, NSW, Australia	101

Gondolier by Alex Malec, Ox and Stone,
  Rochester, NY, USA — 103

Green Dream by Olivia Hu, Sunrise/Sunset,
  Brooklyn, NY, USA — 105

Gringo Negroni by Roberto Giudici, Fluffer Bar,
  Milan, Italy — 108

Gutter Garden, Chris Stanley, Catherine Lombardi,
  New Brunswick, New Jersey, USA. — 110

Havana Daydreaming by Tony Gurdian, Imperial,
  Portland, OR, USA — 113

Heart's Filthy Lesson by Nick Dean, Forte the Restaurant,
  Jamestown, NY, USA — 116

Hidden Dragon by Kris Baljak, Clement in the
  Peninsula Hotel, New York, NY, USA — 118

High Society Cocktail, Verrier Maxime, Pollen Street
  Social, London, UK — 121

Honey Badger by Liam Baer, Fish and Meat, Hong Kong — 123

Isle of Pheasants by Rick Paulger, Michael Symon's Roast,
  Detroit, MI, USA — 125

It Doesn't Take an Empire by Simon Ford, The 86 Co,
  New York, NY — 127

Jasmine Limoncello by Stephen Dennison, Bistro 1860,
  Louisville, KY, USA — 129

Keen-A On You by Donny Clutterbuck, Good Luck,
  Rochester, NY, USA — 131

Killer Queen by Zachary Nelson, The Hammer Bar, Anaheim, CA, USA — 133

King Louie the 4th by Anthony DeSerio, Sticks & Stones, Uncasville, CT, USA — 136

Kirkwall Kelpie by Phil Barlow, The Seamstress, New York, NY, USA — 138

Lime in the Coconut by Andrew Aoun, TAPS Fish House & Brewery, Brea, CA, USA — 141

Lion & Rose by Samuel Tripet, Lily Blacks, Melbourne, Victoria, Australia — 143

Little Dragon by Humberto Marques, CURFEW, Copenhagen, Denmark — 145

Loop by Andreas Sanidiotis, Lost + Found Drinkery, Nicosia, Cyprus — 147

M&M´s by Philipp M. Ernst, Bar 67, Ischgl, Tirol, Austria — 149

Magic Julep by Giuseppe González, Suffolk Arms, New York, NY — 151

Mama Cass by Yuval Soffer, Gatsby, Jerusalem, Israel — 153

Maman Brigitte by Tristan Simon, A La Française, Paris, France — 155

Marmalade Duke by Jonathan Downs, Abode Canterbury Champagne Bar, Canterbury, Kent, UK — 157

Mezcalero by David A. Roth, Cask Bar & Kitchen, New York, NY, USA — 160

MiAmor by Angelika Larkina, EBA Training Center, Tallinn, Harjumaa, Estonia	163
Mime's Well by Chris Grøtvedt, THE THIEF, Oslo, Norway	165
Mumbaiced Tea by Alfonso del Portillo, The Anthologist, London, UK	167
Murder of Goth Chicks by Sean Enright, Tiki Lounge, Pittsburgh, PA	169
Negroni Chinato by Matteo Schianchi, Prospero, Reggio Emilia, Italy	171
New Fashioned by Sonny De Lido, Pizza East Shoreditch, London, England, UK	173
Not Too Sloe by Francesco Lombardi, The Walrus Room, London, England, UK	175
Old Buccaneer by Ivan Di Giovanni, The Walrus Room, London, England, UK	177
Old Fashioned Holiday by Michael Gatlin, Evo, Portland, ME, USA	179
Old Man & The Sea by Andrew Winters, The Blind Rabbit, Anaheim, CA, USA	181
Once Upon A Thyme by Alan Moore, Upstairs @ KinaraKitchen, Dublin, Ireland	183
Peace Offering by Josh Powell, 68 and Boston, London, UK	186
Picasso Sour by Sean Halse, Gold on 27, Dubai, UAE	188

Pilgrim Cocktail by Dale DeGroff, Rainbow Room,
New York, NY, USA — 190

Pine-y the Elder by Andrew Aoun, TAPS Fish House
& Brewery, Brea, CA, USA — 192

Pirate Hook, Justin Southam, ReviveR, Gosford,
New South Wales, Australia — 194

Professor by Boudewijn Mesritz, Tales & Spirits,
Amsterdam, Netherlands — 196

Ready, Steady, Fire! by Ralf Hubbers, Demain, Nijmegen,
Gelderland, Netherlands — 198

Rizal by Jo-Jo Valenzuela, Brine, Fairfax, VA, USA — 200

Seventh Art by Andrew Bennett, The Classroom,
Perth, Australia — 204

Spanish Leather by Courtney Randall, Vito's,
Seattle, WA, USA — 206

Stepford Sister, Jon Hughes, Bramble Bar & Lounge,
Edinburgh, UK — 208

Sunset Strip by Eric Tecosky, Jones Hollywood,
Los Angeles, CA, USA — 210

Tiffin Punch by Wasantha Wikramasinghe, cellar 59,
ART Rotana hotel, Amwaj Island, Bahrain — 212

Two World Hero by Kellie Thorn, Empire State South,
Atlanta, GA, USA — 214

Ultima Palabra by Simone De Luca, The Walrus Room,
London, UK — 216

Voodoo Vie, Bystrik Uko, Oblix Bar, London, UK	218
Walkers N' Bitter by Ryan Haile, Parlour, Oakland, CA, USA	220
We Don't Negotiate With Pirates by Joe Wild, 81 Liverpool Trading Dock, Liverpool, Merseyside, UK	222
White Sazerac by Maroš Dzurus, HIMKOK, Oslo, Norway	224
White Walker, Sky Huo, Earl's Juke Joint, Sydney, NSW, Australia	226
Wild Rover by Jimmy Hillegas, Frolik Kitchen + Cocktails, Seattle, WA, USA	228
Williams Christ Superstar by Björn Bochinski, Lux Bar, Münster, Germany	230
Workers on the Tracks by Luke Andrews, The Whistler, Chicago, IL, USA	232
World Traveler by Frank Caiafa, Peacock Alley, Waldorf-Astoria, New York, NY, USA	234
Yuliya Martini by Andrii Osypchuk, Blasé Dubai, Dubai, UAE	237

INTRODUCTION

This is the fifth and final volume of the *101 Best New Cocktails,* and hopefully you'll all understand that I have great difficulty when it comes to doing the same thing over and over again. I'm pretty amazed that we've managed to put more than a couple of these together.

Onwards and upwards then, for me, and for bartenders all over our luverly planet. You guys have made me so proud to be a bartender that I can't thank you enough for your help, your humor, your creativity, and your giving natures.

I'll be the guy at the end of the bar with a huge smile on his face.

1831

Tim Laferla, Red Bar @ Bam-Bou, London, UK

Tim says: "I created this drink in celebration of Martell cognac's tri-centenary this year, with the vision of becoming a 'future classic.' It's a simple drink with bold flavours that celebrate all the different aroma and taste notes that one looks for in a great VSOP cognac. The name 1831 refers to the year that the house of Martell first released their VSOP expression."

50 ml (1.7 oz) Martell VSOP cognac
20 ml (.66 oz) Cocchi Vermouth de Torino
7.5 ml (.25 oz) Cherry Heering
2 dashes coffee bitters
1 brandied cherry, as garnish.
Stir over ice and strain into a chilled cocktail glass. Add the garnish.

gaz sez: *I get so few cognac-based drinks in my mailbox, and this one, very simple in design, shows a great sense of balance between all four ingredients. And I love that Tim didn't overthink this. He found a formula that worked, and he didn't let it get out of hand.*

Out of interest I also tried this with Dr. Adam Elmegirab's Orinoco Bitters, instead of the coffee bitters, and the result was an entirely new drink, but one that was equally worthy of a chilled glass.

Alcatraz

Christin Wagner, La Petite Grocery, New Orleans, LA, USA

Christin says: "Thanks for trying my drink! I hope you enjoy it as much as I enjoyed creating it."

45 ml (1.5 oz) Tequila Ocho añejo
22.5 ml (.75 oz) Lustau Don Nuño oloroso sherry
15 ml (.5 oz) Suze liqueur
7.5 ml (.25 oz) Del Maguey Vida Mezcal

1 barspoon agave nectar
2 dashes Fee Brothers Aztec Chocolate bitters
1 orange twist

Stir over ice and strain into a chilled rocks glass. Squeeze the twist over the drink and add as garnish.

gaz sez: *Say "ocho" eight times, then run to the liquor store and demand you get your fair share of this remarkable tequila. Cristin showed remarkable balancing techniques when assembling these ingredients, and the use of Suze here is just inspired! Unlike its namesake, though, the Alcatraz Cocktail takes no prisoners. Be warned . . .*

Ambré Carré

Agostino Galli, Lacerba, Milano, Italy

Agostino says: "I created this drink as a thank you for a present from a dear friend of mine, Claudio, who took three bottles of Noilly Prat Ambré from Noilly Prat distillery as a present for the bar staff. He likes France and strong dry drinks, so I also tried to celebrate a really good drink like Vieux Carré and that concept of mixing.

From the Bulleit rye I feel the spices coming to the forefront helped by the sweet cinnamon, candied orange, Sauternes wine of Ambré vermouth. These are followed by hints of peaches and cherries, which work perfectly with the wood taste of Hennessey. that help the strong and long finish. Balsamic notes follow, and the spices in the Absinthe lift above the meld of herbs with a refreshing taste, and give complex aromas. The Gran Classico aromas present a multi-faceted bitter-sweet viscosity, highlighted by sweet rhubarb, the bitter of gentian root and orange peel blend with wormwood, vanilla and resin-y notes. It helps me to balance and alternates between the sweet and bitter. Lemon oil completes the picture."

30 ml (1 oz) Bulleit rye whiskey
30 ml (1 oz) Hennessey cognac
30 ml (1 oz) Noilly Prat Ambré vermouth
10 ml (.33 oz) Gran Classico Bitter
2 dashes The Bitter Truth orange bitters
1 dash Absinthe (Agostino prefers Duplais Verte)

1 lemon twist, as garnish
Stir over ice and strain into a chilled
cocktail glass. Add the garnish.

gaz sez: *Here's one of those recipes that doesn't make a great deal of sense on paper, but drinks beautifully in the glass. Make me just one more, please . . .*

An Offer He Couldn't Refuse

Jason Simplot, Suite 410, Seattle, WA, USA

Jason says: "A highly aromatic grappa cocktail, everything here just loves to swim around together. All of these ingredients are pretty good buddies. The gin and Strega take the astringent quality out of the Grappa and the Vermouth just sings, filling your nose before you drink."

30 ml (1 oz) Candolini Grappa Ruta
30 ml (1 oz) Damrak gin
15 ml (.5 oz) Strega
15 ml (.5 oz) La Quintinye Vermouth Royal blanc

4 healthy dashes Regans' Orange Bitters No. 6

1 edible purple Bachelor Button flower, as garnish

Stir over ice until nice and cold. Strain into a chilled coupe and add the garnish.

gaz sez: *I think that Jason says it all here—this is a finely-balanced aromatic cocktail that, to steal from whoever first said this, "goes down singing hymns." We can learn much from Jason's use of grappa in this cocktail—he tamed it, he calmed it, and yet it still shines right on through. Tip o' the hat to you, sir.*

Angel's Share

Marcus Henriksson, Brooms & Hatches, Oslo, Norway

Marcus says: "I have always been fascinated by the process that occurs during the barrel aging, called the angel's share, when some percent of the spirit is lost to evaporation. There's something almost poetic about it.

The drink is inspired by the classic Rusty Nail and the beautifully named Kiss From Heaven.

While trying to write the recipe down I recalled reading about something called whiskey barrel aged bitters (from the book Bitters by Brad Thomas Parsons), and I wrote it in immediately. And luckily, after trying it out, to me it worked out fine! The idea with the addition of the bitters was to give the drink a strong connection or 'red line' with the whisk(e)y (since Drambuie is a whisky-based liqueur).

Oban 14 Year Old gives a nice character and was my choice after some try outs with this drink. It also works really well with Japanese single malts from Hibiki and Yamazaki and with more peaty whiskies like Talisker or Islay single malts as well, for those who like a rougher kind of drink.

The choice of vermouth was Noilly Prat (though others may as well work out fine), partly to make a connection with the process and name of the drink. The angel's share seems to play an important part in the making of Noilly Prat: During the aging process the wine is aged outdoors, which encourages nature to weave its magic with the influence of the four seasons, so the angel's share is four times greater due to this than if the wines were to be aged in an indoor cellar.

It is said that when Louis Noilly got the question how he could allow for so much of his wine to evaporate in the sun, his answer was something like, 'I want to give a share to the angels (or a taste to the angels)'."

> 45 ml (1.5 oz) Oban 14 Year Old single malt scotch whisky
> 20 ml (.66 oz) Noilly Prat sweet vermouth
> 20 ml (.66 oz) Drambuie
> 2 to 3 dashes Fee Brothers Whiskey Barrel Aged bitters
> 1 lemon twist, as garnish
> Stir over ice and strain into a chilled sherry goblet. Add the garnish.

gaz sez: *I love Oban. I've been a big fan of this salty dram for a few decades now, and I've seldom seen it put to good use in the cocktail world, but Marcus has nailed it here. The bitters are a nice touch, too.*

Apple of My IPA

Dustin Adams, The Cellar, Fullerton, CA, USA

Dustin says: "I decided to create an approachable beer cocktail because our Orange County patrons are still kind of new to the idea. Now that we're in fall, what better beer to use than an IPA? The pineyness of the beer screams fall to me and I decided on a cider-esque cocktail, but not a warm one because here in Southern California we don't really have a fall and barely a winter, so not everyone really wants a warm drink. So far we've had nothing but rave reviews. The balance between the softness of the Calvados and the sweetness of the cinnamon play well with the in-your-face notes of the allspice and the IPA. It's Southern California's fall in a glass."

45 ml (1.5 oz) Busnel calvados
22.5 ml (.75 oz) Cinnamon Syrup*
15 ml (.5 oz) fresh lemon juice
7.5 ml (.25 oz) St. Elizabeth Allspice Dram
75 ml (2.5 oz) Drake's IPA
3 green apple slices on a pick, as garnish
Grating of fresh cinnamon, as garnish

Lightly shake all ingredients except IPA with ice in a shaker (you don't want too much dilution). Strain into a chilled cocktail glass and add the IPA and garnishes.

*Cinnamon Syrup: Crush 3 sticks Ceylon cinnamon and combine in a saucepan with 240 ml (1 cup) water and 400 g (2 cups) sugar. Bring to a simmer, take off heat, and let sit for at least an hour. Then fine-strain and bottle.

gaz sez: *This is a great use of ale in a cocktail, and Dustin balances everything very nicely, indeed. Apple of my IPA is perfect for the December holidays, too. I must remember that.*

Backyard Barbecue

Paulina Swan, ROUX, Rochester, NY, USA

Laphroaig 10 Year Old scotch whisky, as a rinse
45 ml (1.5 oz) Plymouth gin
15 ml (.5 oz) Cynar
15 ml (.5 oz) Salers aperitif
22.5 ml (.75 oz) fresh lemon juice
15 ml (.5 oz) Squid Ink Syrup*
1 egg white
3 dashes Peychaud's bitters

1 rosemary sprig, as garnish

Rinse a chilled coupe with the scotch. Combine remaining ingredients and dry shake for about 10 seconds, then add ice and shake 15 seconds more. Double-strain into the coupe and add the garnish.

*Squid Ink Syrup: Combine 240 ml (1 cup) water and 200 g (1 cup) sugar to a boil. Take it off the heat and whisk in 3 tablespoons squid ink.

gaz sez: *This isn't the sort of recipe that normally catches my eye, mainly cos I'm a bit of a lazy bastard, and the Backyard Barbecue is a trifle complicated to put together. However, the mention of a Laphroaig rinse got my attention, as did the Peychaud's bitters, so I bit the bullet and took this baby out for dinner and a movie. Got a home run on the first date, too . . .*

BB King

Julian Serna, The Lo & Behold Group, Singapore

50 ml (1.7 oz) Banana Jack Daniel's*

10 ml (.33 oz) Smoked Maple Syrup**

4 drops Bitter End Memphis Barbeque bitters

Stir over ice and strain into crystal cut tumbler over a large block of ice.

*Banana Jack Daniel's: Use 3 peeled bananas per 750-ml bottle of Jack Daniel's and let infuse for 3 days. Reserve infused bananas for another use. (We made Banana Whisky Sorbet and used as a garnish.)

**Smoked Maple Syrup: Infuse use quality Canadian maple syrup with hickory chip smoke.

gaz sez: *Just when you thought that drinks couldn't get any stranger . . . God only know what goes on in the mind of Julian Serna, but this drink proves that, as weird as the recipe looks, he sure as heck knows what he's doing. You're a brave man, sir. And talented, too!*

Bebe Lyon

Mary White, Palmer & Co., Sydney, NSW, Australia

Mary says: "Named after the 1920s actress and dancer. Vivacious and delicate; surely a hellcat on the dance floor, she holds a dehydrated flower."

45 ml (1.5 oz) Beefeater gin
20 ml (.66 oz) Persimmon and Vanilla Shrub*
15 ml (.5 oz) yellow Chartreuse
1 sprig dehydrated baby's breath, as garnish

Shake over ice and double-strain into a chilled cocktail glass. Add the garnish.

*Persimmon and Vanilla Shrub: Mix 14 to 15 persimmons (roughly cut into small pieces), 5 kg (11 pounds) caster (also called superfine) sugar, and 10 sliced vanilla pods, ensuring fruit is fully coated with sugar. Allow to sit in fridge for 1 day (harder Fuji persimmons may require an extra day) or until the sugar has drawn most of the liquid from fruit. Add 5 L (5.25 quarts) apple cider vinegar and heat slightly to dissolve sugar. Strain and enjoy.

gaz sez: *I believe that the Bebe Lyon to whom Mary refers here was originally known as Bebe Daniels, a child star who, in 1910, at the age of 9, appeared as Dorothy in a short film,* The Wonderful Wizard of Oz. *After appearing in a number of films, she married actor Ben Lyon in 1930, and five years later they moved to England. In the 1950s Ben and Bebe starred in a radio sit-com called Life with the Lyons, and I actually remember listening to that show as a kid. Thanks for the memory, Mary! And thanks for this drink, too.*

It's been a while since I made shrub, and I admit that I cut the recipe down when I made this one, us-

ing approximately 25% of each ingredient. It was worth the trouble. This is a fabulous creation, and the Yellow Chartreuse, even though it's in such a small quantity, plays a major role in the Bebe Lyon cocktail. I'll be serving these nxt time we have guests over.

Bee Negroni

Maxime Verrier, HIMKOK, Oslo, Norway

Maxime says: "I love drinks that tell you a story. This drink is inspired by the bees producing the beeswax we use to infuse our gin. This Negroni represents the journey of nature and hard work of bees.

"St. Germain will bring the elderflower blossoms' touch, then sloe gin the berries notes (cherry and plum) and the beeswax-infused gin will bring the final touch. Campari for bitterness and Antica Formula for the rich spices notes.

"This Negroni will bring you, from flowers to fruit, honey and spices, with a much needed bitter character."

10 ml (.33 oz) sloe gin
20 ml (.66 oz) Beeswax-Infused Gin*
20 ml (.66 oz) Carpano Antica Formula
15 ml (.5 oz) Campari
1 barspoon St. Germain
1 orange twist, as garnish

Pour all the ingredients in a rock glass. Fill with ice and stir gently. Add the garnish.

*Beeswax-Infused Gin: Combine 20 g (about 1.5 tablespoons) of beeswax and 1 liter of London dry gin. Cook sous vide or in a closed container at 40°C (105°F) for 6 hours.

gaz sez: *Maxime and the crew at HIMKOK sent me a sample of their beeswax-infused gin so I could try this drink, so I awarded extra points for effort here! The extra points weren't needed, though—the cocktail is superb, and stands tall on its own merits.*

Black Ruby

Serena Bass, Lido, New York, NY, USA

45 ml (1.5 oz) tequila
60 ml (2 oz) Ginger Lime Simple Syrup*
30 ml (1 oz) blackcurrant puree
1 teaspoon sriracha
45 ml (1.5 oz) Club soda
1 lime wedge, as garnish

Mix the ingredients in a rocks glass, stirring well. Add ice and top with soda. Add the garnish.

*Ginger Lime Simple Syrup: Combine 50 g (1 cup) peeled and sliced fresh ginger, 200 g (1 cup) sugar, and 240 ml (1 cup) fresh lime juice in a medium STAINLESS STEEL pan and bring to simmer.

Cool for two minutes then blend very well. Strain, pressing through the sieve, and reserve the liquid. Store covered and refrigerated.

gaz sez: *Be very very careful with the sriracha sauce in this recipe—it can overtake the whole darned drink. When made properly, though, The Black Ruby is a drink of great beauty, and it displays creativity and a great understanding of ingredients on the part of Executive Chef Serena Bass. Quite simply, this is a masterpiece.*

Blind Spot

Danny Whelan, Kelvingrove Café, Glasgow, Scotland, UK

40 ml (1.35 oz) rye genever (Danny uses Zuidam Rogge)
25 ml (.8 oz) fresh lime juice
20 ml (.66 oz) pineapple syrup
10 ml (.33 oz) Orange Colombo
3 dashes Dead Rabbit Orinoco bitters
1 pineapple leaf, as garnish

Shake over ice and strain through Hawthorne and tea strainers into a chilled, elegant stemmed glass. Add the garnish.

gaz sez: *One of the most unusual drinks I've sampled all year, and it seemed to appear out of nowhere. Must have been in my blind spot . . . Great drink, Danny!*

Bogmyrtle Blazer

Jesper Strauss, Le Mouton Noir + Tall Guy Spirits, Copenhagen, Denmark

Jesper says: "In the process of stringing together our winter menu, I wanted to do a warm drink outside the traditional glögg, hot toddy and hot buttered rum. Blazers are a very new style of drink for me to be creating, but this turned out to be very popular from the start. The combination is a mix of sweet, boozy and spiced.

"The ambition was to create a drink with a lot of power, sweetness and maintain the flavor of the aquavit."

A Word of Caution: This drink involves setting alcohol on fire and pouring it from one fireproof container to another. It can be as dangerous as it sounds. Practice with water until you feel comfortable with the action, make sure your service area (including floor) are free of anything flammable, and always have a fire extinguisher close at hand.

40 ml (1.35 oz) Aalborg Porse Snaps (bogmyrtle aquavit)
20 ml (.66 oz) Drambuie
5 ml (.16 oz or 1 teaspoon) La Fée Absinthe
2 dashes Mozart chocolate bitters
1 lemon twist, as garnish

Using 2 tankards suitable for mixing Blue Blazers, combine all ingredients in one tankard and ignite. Carefully blaze the drink 12 to 15 times between the two tankards. Extinguish the flame completely. Strain into a vintage tea cup and add the garnish.

gaz sez: *Bogmyrtle Rules. Okay? This is a seriously fabulous quaff, and I predict we'll see far more aquavits in new cocktails before too very long. Jesper: This one makes me think that you might actually know what you're doing . . .*

Bonfire Banger

Benji Ryde, RYND Bar & Kitchen, Reading, Berkshire, UK

Benji says: "How to create a bonfire atmosphere? Wrap flash string around the coupe at the stem and run it through the back of a coaster made of sculpted foil. After you've served the drink, use a smoking gun to add Applewood smoke, then light the flash string. Serve with toasted marshmallows."

45 ml (1.5 oz) Talisker 10 Year Old Scotch whisky
15 ml (.5 oz) Bénédictine
10 ml (.33 oz) Cherry Heering
4 dashes Angostura bitters

2 dashes Fee Brothers Black Walnut bitters

1 orange twist, as garnish

Stir over ice and strain into a chilled coupe. Add the garnish.

gaz sez: *For those who aren't aware of Bonfire Night, it rolls around every year on November 5th in the UK (mainly in England, I think). Bonfires are built, and effigies of Guy Fawkes, a man involved in a plot to blow up the Houses of Parliament in 1605, are burned at the stake. Those Brits have long memories! And the name of this drink—Bonfire Banger—refers to exploding fireworks that are commonly ignited on Bonfire Night, as it's commonly known.*

This drink is a beauty, and its composition is right up my alley. I love every single ingredient in this baby, but I must single out the Fee Brothers Black Walnut bitters as stealing the show here—they bring everything together in complete harmony. The dastardly Joe Fee knows what he's doing!

Bramble On

Anthony DeSerio and Ryan Henry Tunnacliffe, Sticks and Stones, Uncasville, CT, USA

Anthony says: "This is a 'you can add one more interesting ingredient to a classic' cocktail. Once again, we at Sticks and Stones were experimenting with a gin cocktail for a special. The team loves Brambles. Ryan Tunnacliffe and I pulled this together, knowing we just got some fresh blackberries in stock. But Ryan said we needed a twist, so we agreed on a flamed rosemary garnish. To which I thought, 'Why don't we add the rosemary to the syrup, too?' This way we would have the aromatic flavor in the drink as well. Ryan said give it a shot ... I did and it worked! We sold out in one night. Sometimes a little extra goes a long way in a drink that can stand on its own."

45 ml (1.5 oz) Plymouth gin
22.5 ml (.75 oz) Blackberry-Rosemary Syrup*
15 ml (.5 oz) fresh lemon juice
1 blackberry, as garnish
1 rosemary sprig, as garnish

Shake over ice and strain into an ice-filled rocks glass. Add the blackberry garnish. Dip the rosemary in Absinthe and stand it up in the cocktail. Light it, give it a second or two to burn, then gently blow out the flame over the top of the cocktail for added aromatics.

*Blackberry-Rosemary Syrup: Combine 200 g (1 cup) granulated sugar, 150 g (1 cup) blackberries, and 240 ml (1 cup) water in a saucepan over medium-low heat. Muddle berries and mix to dissolve the sugar. Bring up heat to just under a boil and add 4 to 5 fresh rosemary sprigs. Stir for 1 minute and remove from heat. Let mixture steep and cool to room temperature. Strain out solids through a tea strainer and store in a refrigerator-safe container.

gaz sez: *The original Bramble, of course, is a modern-day classic created by London Legendary bartender, Dick Bradsell, and it really is a masterpiece. This twist on Dick's drink is also a fabulous drink, and the addition of rosemary in the syrup, and perhaps just as importantly, as a flamed garnish that's been dipped in absinthe, is simply inspired. Congrats, Gents, you've done yourselves proud.*

Britoni

Antonio Anzelmo, Smith & Wollensky, London, UK

Antonio says: "Nothing can beat a good classic Negroni, but this one is definitely a good alternative!"

40 ml (1.35 oz) Kamm & Sons
(*see gaz sez*)
35 ml (1.17 oz) Cynar
15 ml (.5 oz) Kingston Black apple aperitif
2 drops Angostura bitters

2 ml (.5 teaspoon) Bob's Liquorice bitters

1 grapefruit twist, as garnish

Stir over ice and strain into an old-fashioned glass over cube ice. Add the garnish.

gaz sez: *Kamm & Sons isn't available in the USA so my unpaid Brit tester tried this drink first, and she was so impressed that she sent me a sample in a plain wrapper, and boy was she right. This is an outstanding creation, and it's hard to say where the drink begins, and where it ends. Each and every ingredient seems to get a chance to sing a solo as this baby fills your mouth with music. Incredible.*

Burnt Brandy & Peach

Jon Yeager, PourTaste, Nashville, TN, USA

Jon says: "This is a modern rendition of Jerry Thomas' drink by the same name. His method was essentially cooking brandy and peaches together, to be served in a mug. This rendition enables a bartender to make and serve this individually."

45 ml (1.5 oz) Delord Napoleon armagnac
30 ml (1 oz) Carpano Antica Formula
15 ml (.5 oz) Massenez crème de pêche
2 dashes Angostura bitters

7.5 ml (.25 oz) Laird's Straight apple brandy

Stir the armagnac, vermouth, crème de pêche, and bitters over ice for 20 seconds, then pour into an individual wine decanter. Rinse a coupe with the apple brandy (do not discard) and ignite. Slowly pour the chilled cocktail into the flaming coupe and serve.

gaz sez: *This is absolutely beautiful. Deserves a standing ovation. I'll be serving these at parties for sure.*

Charlie Wallbanger

Brian Nixon, McClellan's Retreat, Washington, DC, USA

Brian says: "We came up with this drink for our 'Fern Bar' throwback menu. The way the Galliano and Aquavit play together was good, but the Corrected Orange Juice and cardamom bitters really made all the flavors work together. People liked it so much I had to order more Galliano, something I never thought I'd have to do."

45 ml (1.5 oz) Linie aquavit
90 ml (3 oz) Corrected Orange Juice*
2 dashes Scrappy's cardamom bitters

30 ml (1 oz) Galliano

1 orange slice, as garnish

Build in a Collins glass with ice. Float Galliano and add the garnish.

*Corrected Orange Juice: Mix 16 grams (1 tablespoon) citric acid and 10 grams (2 teaspoons) malic acid with 1 liter (1 generous quart) fresh orange juice.

gaz sez: *Tee Hee! If you ever wondered what an empty bottle of Galliano looked like, now you have the answer. And this riff on the Harvey Wallbanger is just terrific. Back in the 70s we used tequila instead of vodka to make Freddie Fudpuckers, and they weren't too shabby, either.*

Chartreuse Cobbler

Oron Lerner, French 57, Tel Aviv, Israel

Oron says: "This drink was made on the fly one night when I realized I hadn't anything prepared but the bar was slammed. Its intuitively simple recipe made me dismiss it as merely a crowd pleaser (as if pleasing the crowds is a 'merely'). Two years later, I am unable to take it off the menu with guests still coming in to ask for it again and again. It was only a remark by a guest that made me realize that the Chartreuse Cobbler is our basil smash, it has legacy, endurance. More often than not bartenders look for what excites them and miss out on what excites their guests, who aren't into mezcals, amaros, and rare gins but into what was once considered 'wholesome flavors' and is now looked down on, at times, as mainstream. Delicious, simple in recipe, complex in flavor, elegant, and above all, long lasting."

5 fresh mint leaves
45 ml (1.5 oz) Beefeater 24 gin

15 ml (.5 oz) green Chartreuse
30 ml (1 oz) fresh lime juice
20 ml (.66 oz) simple syrup
1 fresh rosemary sprig, as garnish

Fill and old-fashioned glass with ice and set aside. Spank the mint and add to a shaker with ice and the remaining ingredients. Shake well and hard. Before straining, dip the rosemary in green Chartreuse, light it on fire, and place in the glass. Strain the cocktail over the burning rosemary, thus extinguishing the fire and filling the glass with rosemary and Chartreuse smoke.

gaz sez: *Oron's comments here ring so very true. I nearly passed this recipe over as being "one of the crowd," but then I started wondering how well Chartreuse and Beefeater 24 would pal-up to each other, and guess what—they're life-long pals. If this one's a crowd-pleaser you can count me in as one of the crowd.*

Colleen Bawn Knickebein

Frederic Yarm, Loyal Nine, Cambridge, MA, USA

Fred says: "I was introduced to the Colleen Bawn by Misty Kalkofen at Green Street Grill before her days at Drink and beyond; this gem from Edward Spencer's The Flowing Bowl quickly became one of my favorite flips. The concept of Knickebeins—quirky layered drinks taken in a prescribed methodology as an almost rite of passage given the unbroken egg yolk aspect—came to me via John Gertsen at No. 9 Park. I thought, 'What if you could combine the wonders of a flip with the mystery of a pousse-café in the form of a Knickebein?' Then I made it and wondered how could something be this awesome!"

1 egg

15 ml (.5 oz) Bénédictine

15 ml (.5 oz) yellow Chartreuse

15 ml (.5 oz) straight rye whiskey

Freshly grated cinnamon and nutmeg, as garnish

Separate the egg, being careful not to break the yolk. Beat the egg white into a stiff meringue (my preferred method is a shaker tin with a balled up Hawthorne strainer spring).

Layer the Bénédictine and then the Chartreuse using the back of a spoon or the flat end of a Bonzer spoon handle (the densities are close enough that this part might be difficult or at least a little blurred transition-wise). Carefully float the yolk using the bowl of a cocktail spoon. Layer the whiskey as done with the liqueurs. Top with meringue and add the garnish.

Drink in the methodology prescribed by Leo Engel in 1878 in his book *American and Other Drinks*:

Pass the glass under the Nostrils and Inhale the Flavour -- Pause.

Hold the glass perpendicularly, close under your mouth, open it wide, and suck the froth by drawing a Deep Breath. – Pause again.

Point the lips and take one-third of the liquid contents remaining in the glass without touching the yolk. – Pause once more.

Straighten the body, throw the head backward, swallow the contents remaining in the glass all at once, at the same time breaking the yolk in your mouth.

gaz sez: *Fred sent this recipe to me after I asked, on Facebook, for new Pousse-Café style drinks, and I was so taken with this formula that I decided to add it to my 101BNC list this year. Let's just say that the combination of Bénédictine, Chartreuse, and rye, is right up my alley.*

Fred seems to have a bit of a fixation on Knickebeins! And it's a category of drinks, created, as far as I know, by Leo Engel, author of American & Other Drinks *and bartender at the American Bar in the Criterion Hotel in London, that I'm guilty of ignoring for the most part, but this variation is simply stunning. And it's bound to impress guests. I'd better take another looks at these Knickebeins.*

Devil's Pitchfork

Ted Kilgore, Planter's House, Saint Louis, MO, USA

Ted says: "As I was catching up on some emails and checking newsletters I rarely have time to read any more now that I am an owner, a Difford's Guide article about gentian root liqueurs piqued my interest. In this post it was revealed that the tool they used to harvest the roots is called a Devil's Pitchfork. I of course thought there needs to be a drink with that name and it needs to be with an unruly amount of *gentian liqueur. After sending for test subjects to try the abomination in my brain, the Devil's Pitchfork was agreed upon. I now promise to stop bothering you with weird evil drinks that cause depravity."*

30 ml (1 oz) Rittenhouse 100-proof rye whiskey (oh come on Gaz, you knew it was going to start that way, didn't you?)

22.5 ml (.75 oz) Suze liqueur

22.5 ml (.75 oz) Salers aperitif

7.5 ml (.25 oz) Joseph Cartron crème de cerise (or Cherry Heering)

2 dashes Bittercube Corazòn bitters

1 long grapefruit twist, as garnish (see Note)

1 cherry, as garnish

Stir over ice and strain into a highball glass with a big cube of ice. Add the garnishes.

Note: Trim one end of the grapefruit twist into 3 points to resemble pitchfork tines. We use custom ice cylinders and wrap the twist up the side and lay it across the top.

gaz sez: *I'll be uber-sad if Ted Kilgore ever stops bothering me with weird evil drinks that cause depravity. It's what he does best. Good to see you're still a crazy bastard, Ted, and that your current creations are so well put together. I'd never expect less from you.*

Do-Right

Jared Fischer, Clement in the Peninsula Hotel, New York, NY, USA

Jared says: "You recently featured our creation The Hidden Dragon, with a lament about the complexity in production of some modern cocktails. By sheer coincidence, at the time the feature came out, we were creating a cocktail that does the opposite, something that provides an original flavor profile but could be produced with standard ingredients found in any bar in the world—a potential future classic. We also wanted to do it with spirits that don't always get enough love. After homing in on the right spirits and adjusting the proportions, the Do-

Right was born. Its base is Canadian, its color is red, and the creators are old enough to appreciate *Rocky & Bullwinkle*."

> 45 ml (1.5 oz) Crown Royal
> 30 ml (1 oz) Pimm's No. 1 Cup
> 22.5 ml (.75 oz) Cherry Heering
> 3 dashes orange bitters (we use Regans' No. 6)
> 1 orange twist, as garnish
>
> Stir over ice and strain into a chilled rocks glass. (As with a Manhattan, a Do-Right may be served up or on the rocks, but I prefer it up in a rocks glass.) Rim the glass with oil from the twist, then add as garnish.

gaz sez: *Right up my alley, this one. And I already have me a do right all day woman, so I guess I'm set. Seriously, though, it's the Pimm's that brings this drink together, and she does it with great style, too.*

Dom's Bomb

Ankit Dabral, Conservatory, Melbourne, Australia.

Ankit says: "The whole idea for this drink originated from a documentary I watched on the Ancient Spice Route. I wanted to connect dots and merge two of my favorite eras, the ancient world and Middle Ages, and combine two distinct culture of that time, East and West. I based most of the elements in the cocktail on the ancient spice route, where the glass represents

Ancient Egypt, coffee from Yemen/Arabia, rosemary from Europe, spices and sugar from subcontinent and orange from the Orient. I needed to give Dom Bénédictine the credibility for the drink, as the idea originated only on the basis for a Dom Bénédictine-based drink, and hence the name."

10 g (about 4 teaspoons) ground cinnamon

20 g (1.5 tablespoons) caster sugar, plus more for garnish

1 whole orange, as garnish

2 to 4 whole rosemary sprigs, as garnish

30 ml (1 oz) Rosemary-Infused Tanqueray*

30 ml (1 oz) Dom Bénédictine

30 ml (1 oz) Spiced Coffee Syrup**

30 ml (1 oz) fresh orange juice

Combine cinnamon and sugar and rim an old-fashioned glass with the mixture. Fill with crushed ice.

To make the garnish, cut an orange into 1-cm (.5-inch) slices (preferably through meat slicer). Place a small rosemary sprig over each orange slice and sprinkle with caster sugar. Use a blow torch to caramelize the sugar so the rosemary sticks to the orange.

Shake vigorously with ice until tin is frosted. Strain into the prepared glass and add the garnish.

*Rosemary-Infused Tanqueray: Add 2 to 3 rosemary sprigs to a bottle of Tanqueray and let it sit for around 2 to 3 days before use. Strain through a double layer of dampened cheesecloth, and return the gin to a bottle.

**Spiced Coffee Syrup: Combine 100 ml (3.4 oz) water and 50 g (.25 cup) sugar with whole spices (such as cinnamon, cardamom, star anise, and cloves) and boil until mixture is viscous enough for a 1:1 ratio. Add 120 ml (4 oz) brewed espresso and let it cool. Add warm water if the liquid is too thick but do not thin down too much. Leave the spices in the mixture for more taste and aroma. Refrigerate the syrup for 2 to 3 days and strain before use.

gaz sez: *Jeez, I hardly know where to begin with this one. Let me just say that it's a quietly comforting drink. It's a quaff to sip whilst considering the complexities of life. There's just something about this baby that makes me want to smile quietly to myself.*

Dye House

Samuel Nelis, Waterworks Food + Drink, Winooski, Vermont, USA

Samuel says: "This Clover Club variation is named after the area of an old textile mill where the restaurant is now located. I always thought it would be a good name for a bar, but since the name of the restaurant was already chosen I figured next best thing would be to name one of our signature cocktails after it."

45 ml (1.5 oz) gin (Beefeater)
15 ml (.5 oz) fino sherry
22.5 ml (.75 oz) fresh lemon juice
22.5 ml (.75 oz) Blueberry Syrup*
1 egg white
Brandied blueberries, as garnish

Dry-shake, then add ice and shake again. Double-strain into a chilled coupe and add the garnish.

*Blueberry Syrup: Mix 1.8 kg (4 lb) chopped blueberries with 1.6 kg (3.5 lb) sugar and let stand overnight. Pour 1.4 L (1.5 quarts) warm simple syrup into the mixture and shake until the sugar dissolves, then strain.

gaz sez: *I sure as heck loves me some blueberries, I does, but it's the marriage of Beefeater gin and fino sherry that really piqued my interest in this drink. It's a match made in heaven, methinks! Nicely thought out, Samuel!*

Early Evening Fizz

Nick Caputo, Sovereign Loss, London, UK

Nick says: "This drink was created to achieve two things: To make a really accessible yet delicious Chartreuse cocktail and also to bring as much through of the armagnac too (which is overlooked as a cocktail ingredient). Chartreuse somehow just works as an equal-parts ingredient—more than you would think—and the salt in this drink stops the texture from becoming too cloyingly sweet. It's refreshing and simple yet uses overlooked ingredients with a complex balance of ingredients. Plus who doesn't like a good fizz from time to time?"

25 ml (.8 oz) Janneau VSOP armagnac
25 ml (.8 oz) Plymouth sloe gin
25 ml (.8 oz) green Chartreuse
25 ml (.8 oz) fresh lemon juice
12.5 ml (.4 oz) simple syrup (2:1)
1 pinch sea salt
1 egg white
60 ml (2 oz) soda water (plus more to top off, if needed)
1 lemon twist
1 lemon wedge and cherries, on a pick, as garnish

Dry-shake, then add ice and shake again. Serve Ramos gin fizz style—no ice with a big froth. To achieve this, pour soda slowly into a chilled highball glass at a 45° angle (this keeps as much carbonation as possible). Then start straining the drink over the soda quickly and get gradually slower to build the froth. Squeeze the twist over the drink, then discard. Add the garnishes. Serve with a straw, which should stand straight in the glass due to the foam.

gaz sez: *Thank God someone's using armagnac. I love armagnac. It's a completely different animal than cognac, and I'd never dare to attempt to compare the two. Nick took some chances on this one, and his derring-do paid off handsomely. Well done, sir. I needed a good excuse to raid the armagnac . . .*

El Diablo Loco

Giuseppe Serra, The Palomar Restaurant, London, England, UK

Giuseppe says: "I created the 'El Diablo Loco' after having a cherry chocolate with my espresso during a dinner with friends; I got inspired by those flavours, and wanted to replicate them into a drink.

"I decide to use El Dorado 8 year rum as I think it works well with the idea of an after-dinner cocktail. I then infused the Antica Formula vermouth with coffee, I also used Cherry Heering and finished with a bit of Mezcal Chichicapa, to give a bit of smokiness to the cocktail, as I think it works well with coffee. As garnish, a classic truffle chocolate completed in a unique result which the idea was. SALUTE!"

40 ml (1.35 oz) El Dorado 8 Year Old rum

10 ml (.33 oz) Coffee-Infused Carpano Antica Formula*

10 ml (.33 oz) Cherry Heering

10 ml (.33 oz) Del Maguey Chichicapa Mezcal

1 Truffle Chocolate, as garnish**

Stir over ice and strain into a chilled cocktail glass. Add the garnish.

*Coffee-Infused Carpano Antica Formula: Infuse 50 g (about 6 tablespoons) of ground coffee in 375 ml of vermouth for 20 minutes. Strain through a double layer of cheesecloth.

**Truffle Chocolate: Combine 300 g (10.5 oz) of 54% chocolate and 125 g (.5 cup) of whipping cream in a saucepan over medium heat. Bring just to a boil. Add 40 g (about 3 tablespoons) of sugar, then mix all with 15 g (1 tablespoon) of butter. Store everything in the fridge for 24 hours, then shape into truffles about 5 grams each.

gaz sez: *Jeez this was a pain to put together, but the resultant drink makes it all worth while. Giuseppe makes his own chocolate truffles for the garnish, but for the sake of ink and space we're going to let you buy a good commercial brand. Don't miss out on the garnish, though. After the chocolate has soaked in this spectacular drink, it's a very beautiful thing in the mouth. Promise.*

Élysée Treaty

Ivan Mandaric, Oxbo Urban Bar & Grill, DoubleTree by Hilton Hotel, Zagreb, Croatia

Ivan says: "Eighteen years after the end of World War II, in 1963, French Republic president Charles de Gaulle and German chancellor Konrad Adenauer signed a treaty of friendship between France and Germany called the Élysée Treaty. That event inspired me to make this well-balanced cocktail for Hilton Worldwide autumn cocktail competition. The two main ingredients come from France and Germany and go so well together due to their aroma and taste characteristics. It seems like they signed their own treaty! Taste is a bit darker with chocolate and orange notes, with slightly sweet and bitter notes. This cocktail is an excellent choice to enjoy during a rainy autumn day, watching the leaves coming off the trees. Although it is served cold, the taste itself gives you a feeling of warming up your entire body. It can be recommended as after-dinner drink (digestive) or just enjoyed at the bar to make your day!"

2 wide strips orange zest
40 ml (1.35 oz) Martell VS cognac
20 ml (.66 oz) Jägermeister
20 ml (.66 oz) sugar syrup (1:1)
4 to 5 drops Bitter Truth orange bitters
(or any other orange bitters)
1 orange twist, as garnish
Shake vigorously with a lot of ice in order to chill it properly and incorporate the essential oils from the orange zest into

the cocktail. Double-strain into a chilled cocktail glass and add the garnish.

gaz sez: *I think that many people are aware that I'm a huge Jägermeister freak, and I have been for many years, so this recipe jumped out at me as soon as I glanced at it. The drink is simply marvelous, and I encourage everyone to serve it to folk who don't understand just how marvelously intricate is Jägermeister, and how much character it can add to a cocktail if used judiciously.*

Final Straw

Geoff Fewell, Boilermaker House, Melbourne, Victoria, Australia

Geoff says: "Enjoy—there is no garnish by the way. Please don't fiddle with the recipe.... No Ellen and I may buy you a drink."

20 ml (.66 oz) Laphroaig Quarter Cask scotch whisky
20 ml (.66 oz) Bénédictine
20 ml (.66 oz) Chartreuse M.O.F.
20 ml (.66 oz) fresh lemon juice

Shake over ice and double-strain into a chilled Nick & Nora glass or coupette.

gaz sez: *Sorry to say, Geoff, that I had no Chartreuse M.O.F. (Cuvée des Meilleurs Ouvriers de France Sommeliers), so I used the regular yellow Chartreuse when I tested this, and I must say that it's a delightful quaff, indeed. Nice use of Laphroaig in this one, sir!*

Five Finger Death Punch

David Adams, The Dead Canary, Cardiff, Glamorgan, UK

David says: "After reading through a bunch of Dead Rabbit recipes for 'over the bar punches' I was hungry to create something of my own that I could serve to guests to introduce them to the category. We'd been playing around at work with the idea of creating a 'house whisky blend' that we could serve in a number of classics to industry friends and it just so happened that this blend had just the right level of smokiness and maltiness to make for a really balanced and cracking punch. (We premix the whisky to improve speed of service.) The peach liqueur really adds to the drink and makes it a little more accessible for the general public than a lot of other drinks with a potent whisky base.

"The name Five Finger Death Punch is in reference to the five different whisk(e)ys, the potency of the drink, the heavy metal band, and classic martial arts cinema.

"This drink has quickly become our best seller at The Dead Canary and is a great alternative for those ordering Long Island iced teas purely for the number of different spirits!"

12.5 ml (.42 oz) Buffalo Trace bourbon
12.5 ml (.42 oz) Rittenhouse 100 rye whiskey
12.5 ml (.42 oz) Teeling Single Grain Irish whiskey
12.5 ml (.42 oz) Monkey Shoulder scotch whisky

10 ml (.33 oz) Ardbeg scotch whisky
15 ml (.5 oz) crème de pêche
25 ml (.8 oz) lemon sherbet
25 ml (.8 oz) fresh lemon juice
2 dashes Dr. Adam Elmegirab's Orinoco bitters

Grated nutmeg, as garnish
Shake well and strain into a chilled
punch glass over a large shard of ice.
Add the garnish.

gaz sez: *I must admit that I find the "house blend whiskey" concept a little odd, but that said, David did a great job here, so it's no surprise to me that this drink is a best seller.*

Forged & Bound

Jacques Bezuidenhout, Forgery, San Francisco, CA, USA

52.5 ml (1.75 oz) Wild Turkey 101 rye whiskey
22.5 ml (.75 oz) Amaro Montenegro
7.5 ml (.25 oz) Galliano Ristretto
1 barspoon green Chartreuse
3 dashes Abbott's bitters
1 lemon twist, as garnish

Stir over ice and strain into a chilled Nick & Nora glass. Add the garnish.

gaz sez: *Jacques B gave me a small bottle of pre-made Forged & Bound cocktail at a gathering of booze-hounds when we met up for an afternoon holiday session in Manhattan in December, 2015, and of course I sampled it as soon as I got home. One more cocktail was the last thing I needed that night, but boy, oh boy, was I impressed with this drink. You will be, too. I promise.*

French Old-Fashioned

Pete Volkmar, Gourmet Galley Catering, North Stonington, CT, USA

60 ml (2 oz) Michter's US1 Kentucky Straight Rye Whiskey

7.5 ml (.25 oz) Green Chartreuse

2 dashes Dale DeGroff's Aromatic Bitters

2 dashes Regans' Orange Bitters No.6

1 large orange twist for oil and garnish

Stir all ingredients well over ice and strain into a chilled rocks glass. Optionally, the drink may be mixed and stirred in the glass it will be served in. Bend and squeeze the orange twist, shiny side toward the mixed drink, to release the oil onto the drink's surface. Rub the rim of the glass with the bent orange twist and drop it into the drink. Serve on a cocktail napkin.

gaz sez: *There's something about an Old-Fashioned; a Wicked, Whiskey Old-Fashioned . . . And this one takes the cake as Kentucky meets France in complete harmony, and Dale's bitters and my bitters jump into the fray, too. Nice one, Pete!*

Freshmaker

Eric Grenier, Honor Kitchen & Cocktails, Oakland, CA, USA

45 ml (1.5 oz) Strawberry-Infused Rum*
22.5 ml (.75 oz) fresh lemon juice
22.5 ml (.75 oz) Black Pepper Syrup**
15 ml (.5 oz) Fernet Branca
Cream soda (preferably Hank's Vanilla Cream)
1 mint sprig, as garnish

Shake over ice and strain into an ice-filled collins glass. Top with cream soda and add the garnish.

*Strawberry-Infused Rum: Remove stems and chop 2 pints of ripe strawberries. Place fruit in a wide-mouth mason jar and fill with enough rum (I use El Dorado 3 Year Old) to cover the fruit. Macerate for 3 to 4 days, or to taste. Strain out the solids, being careful not to press on the fruit, and bottle.

**Black Pepper Syrup: Dissolve 200 g (1 cup) granulated sugar into 360 ml (1.5 cups) of water over medium heat. When dissolved, add 10 g (1 tablespoon) cracked black peppercorns and 10 g (1 tablespoon) whole black peppercorns. Let syrup simmer for 20 minutes. Cool and bottle. May be kept up to one month.

gaz sez: *I never needed a gateway to Fernet, personally, but I'm in favor of making new converts to it, and this drink works really well in so many ways. Freshmaker is a very complex drink, and at the same time there's no need to make a fuss over it—just sip and smile. You'll be happy you did.*

Full Blood

Michael Gatlin, Evo, Portland, Maine, USA

Michael says: "I run the bar program at Evo, a Mediterranean restaurant in downtown Portland that specializes in exotic recipes from the Levantine region. In creating the menu my aim was to bring some of the elements from the region and make them accessible to a drinking crowd. The name Full Blood refers to the Sanguinello orange grown in Spain and Sicily."

45 ml (1.5 oz) Metaxa 5 Stars
15 ml (.5 oz) Lillet Rouge
15 ml (.5 oz) blood orange puree
22.5 ml (.75 oz) fresh lemon juice
7.5 ml (.25 oz) Basil Honey Syrup*
Shake over ice and strain into a chilled cocktail glass.
*Basil Honey Syrup: Bring 1 cup honey, 1 cup water, and 12 basil leaves to a simmer and let rest until cool. Strain and refrigerate.

gaz sez: *I've a soft spot in my heart for Metaxa, a sweet, herbal Greek spirit that most folk think of as a brandy, since in the 1970s we used to make Continental Stingers with Metaxa and Galliano, and they went down rather well at the time, though I doubt they'd hold up today. There's no denying that Full Blood is a sweet drink, too, and it's a delightful sweet cocktail that, in my opinion, would sell well in any bar in the world.*

Garrigue

Karim Mehdi, SABA, Dublin, Ireland

Karim says: "This cocktail was inspired by the aromas and flavours of Garrigue (name in French écosystème growing around the Mediterranean Sea) in the south of France, where I spent my childhood. And it helped me get through the final 8 of Bacardi Legacy 2015."

50 ml (1.7 oz) Bacardi Superior rum
20 ml (.66 oz) fresh lemon juice
15 ml (.5 oz) yellow Chartreuse
15 ml (.5 oz) orgeat
Pinch sea salt
1 lemon twist, as garnish
1 dried lavender sprig, as garnish
Shake over ice and fine-strain into a chilled cocktail glass. Add the garnishes.

gaz sez: *Here's a great example of a cocktail created by someone who knows how to perform simple marriage ceremonies without overdoing things. It's a basic formula that comes together beautifully in the glass; the salt adds dimension to the drink, and the lavender is a fabulous aromatic garnish. Nice one, Karim.*

Geraldine's Ginger Fizz

Chris Edwardes, Hidden House, Stari Grad, Croatia

Chris says: "A summer winner that outsold all the other cocktails on our list, created for the lovely Geraldine Coates when she visited Hidden."

4 slices fresh ginger
50 ml (1.7 oz) Beefeater gin
12.5 ml (.42 oz) elderflower liqueur
12.5 ml (.42 oz) elderflower syrup
25 ml (.8 oz) fresh lemon juice
5 turns black pepper
100 ml (3.4 oz) Sprite

1 lemon wheel, as garnish

Muddle the ginger thoroughly in a shaker. Add the remaining ingredients (except the Sprite) and as much ice as possible. Shake like your life depends upon it. Dump into a goblet and add more ice. Top with the Sprite and add the garnish and two straws.

gaz sez: *I love ginger, so this baby got tested quickly, and, as expected, Chris Edwardes did a balancing act that few can even aspire to. (The black pepper brought more than its fair share to this party.) The fact that the drink is dedicated to my Sister in Gin, Geraldine Coates, had nothing to do with my love for this fine quaff. Honest!*

Gilbert

Dushan Zaric, The 86 Co, New York, NY

10 red Concord grapes

30 ml (1 oz) BarSol Pisco Italia
30 ml (1 oz) Chardonnay (lightly oaked)
22.5 ml (.75 oz) fresh lemon juice
15 ml (.5 oz) rich simple syrup (2:1)
3 drops 5-Spice Bitters* (Bar Keep Chinese Bitters are highly recommendable as a substitute)
Champagne grapes, as garnish

Muddle the grapes in a mixing glass. Add ice and the remaining ingredients. Shake hard and double-strain into a cocktail coupe. Add the garnish.

5-Spice Bitters: Using a hand torch, slightly burn 5 large brown sugar cubes. Add them, 2 bottles of overproof rum (such as Goslings 151), two 2-inch pieces of ginger, 4 cinnamon sticks, 65 g (.75 cup) whole cloves, 70 g (.5 cup) Szechuan peppercorns, and 8 star anise pods to a 2-liter Mason jar. Let infuse for 2 weeks in cool, dry, and dark place. Strain and store for use. Yields: 2 liters. Shelf life: forever.

gaz sez: *Trust Dushan Zaric to tease every last nuance out of such an excellent product as BarSol's Italia Pisco, and to do it with such fabulous style. You make me smile, my friend.*

Global Jukebox

Paul Zuber, Bank & Bourbon, Philadelphia, PA, USA

Paul says: "The starting point for my first drink was the desire to harness the refreshing properties of one of summer's great joys, FRESH WATERMELON! As a counterpoint to the cooling fruit, my initial instinct was to use the bold and fiery ANCHO REYES ancho chile liqueur. I chose rum as a base spirit, opting for an aged rum with some barrel influence, and immediately thought to infuse it with some of those delicious, ripe black cherries that I have recently been enjoying so frequently. To get started I stopped off at the market on my way to Bank & Bourbon, in order to pick up some fresh produce.

"With my cherries secure, I found myself driving down the expressway, listening to Pierre Robert on the radio recounting stories of the Live Aid concert which was held at JFK stadium in Philadelphia on July 13, 1985, exactly thirty years prior. While presenting some colorful recollections of the all-day musical event, Pierre mentioned that many concert goers vividly remembered being showered with fire-hoses to combat the sweltering temperatures of the day. Listening to the stories, I thought to myself, 'Is that not a wonderful metaphor for exactly what I am trying to do with this cocktail, dousing the heat of this libation with the cooling waters of melon?' It seemed to me that my intent was indeed quite certain, and I determined at that time to name this drink after the historic concert event which its organizer, Bob Geldof, billed as 'a global jukebox.'"

3 large chunks watermelon, about 2" by 2" each

60 ml (2 oz) Cherry-Infused Rum*

22.5 ml (.75 oz) Ancho Reyes

22.5 ml (.75 oz) Cockburn's LBV port

1 watermelon cube, as garnish

3 brandied cherries, as garnish

Muddle the watermelon chunks in a shaker. Add ice and the remaining ingredients. Shake and double-strain into an ice-filled rocks glass. Add the garnishes.

*Cherry-Infused Rum: Combine 1 part stemmed and pitted ripe cherries, .5 part Appleton or other aged rum, and .5 part Cruzan or other lightly aged rum. Let stand in a sealed container for 3 days. Strain into a clean bottle and seal until needed.

gaz sez: *It's interesting to see this Ancho Reyes liqueur cropping up in quite a few recipes I've seen recently, and I love the fact that bartenders seem to be laboring hard to use it in well-balanced cocktails. Such is the case with the Global Jukebox. It's light, no it isn't, it's spicy, that's not right, either, it's fruity, it's forthright, it's hesitant, it's . . . Oh, you're just gonna have to try one for yourself. You won't regret it. Promise.*

Golden Girls

Yi Chen, Berlyn Restaurant, Brooklyn, NY, USA

Yi says: "I created this cocktail for a love interest who had a particular love for lavender, tequila, and the American television show, The Golden Girls. The show's quartet of women is represented by the color of the tequila and the yellow Chartreuse, and lime, and is appropriately named for the resulting color of the cocktail."

Lavender Sugar*, for glass
60 ml (2 oz) Excellia añejo tequila
22.5 ml (.75 oz) dark agave nectar
22.5 ml (.75 oz) fresh lime juice
15 ml (.5 oz) yellow Chartreuse
4 dashes Scrappy's lavender bitters
1 egg white
Dried lavender buds and Lavender Mist**, as garnishes

Rim a chilled coupe with lavender sugar and set aside.

Dry-shake, then add ice and shake again. Double-strain into the coupe. Sprinkle lavender buds on top, then spray the top of the cocktail three times with lavender mist.

*Lavender Sugar: Grind 5 g (1 tablespoon) of dried lavender buds in a clean coffee grinder for 20 seconds. Pour the ground buds into a medium-mesh strainer (large enough to allow bud essences to sift through, but small enough to catch the buds) over a bowl. Sift by tapping the side of the strainer with a hard object such as a spoon. Discard the whole buds. Pulse 25 g (2 tablespoons) of turbinado sugar in the coffee grinder 6 to 7 times until the sugar granules are loosely broken. Combine well with lavender essence.

**Lavender Mist: In a glass container, infuse 10 g (2 tablespoons) of dried lavender buds into 90 ml (3 oz) of 80-proof vodka. Cover and set aside for two days.

Fine-strain the buds from the vodka and pour the liquid into a small atomizer spray bottle.

gaz sez: *Lavender, lavender, lavender! Reminds me of my Aunt Annie's house, does lavender. I can see her singing some daft old song while Uncle Harry played the upright piano when I was a kid. And lavender was in the air. Anyway, a drink that's so tightly knit, that conjures up such specific memories, deserves a standing ovation, I believe. Brava, Yi Chen! Brava!*

Golden Rose

Anthony Le, O Bar and Dining, Sydney, NSW, Australia

Anthony says: "Summer is here in Australia, the service is crazy and people are impatient. That drives me to make drinks with complexity, yet speedy (which I batched, and stored in the freezer in this case). I also want to show off pisco, as the place is a slightly Peruvian theme. I hope to break of the normality of cocktail that pisco is normally involved, sour, so I made a martini style drink. It's easy enough to trump a white wine on a hot summer night, yet have enough depth for concerned drinker."

Absinthe, as rinse
45 ml (1.5 oz) pisco (preferably Campo de Encanto)
10 ml (.33 oz) Gran Classico Bitter

1 barspoon apricot brandy (preferably Joseph Cartron Abricot)

1 barspoon grappa (preferably Domenis Storica, or any floral, fruity grappa)

3 drops rosewater

1 orange twist

Rinse a chilled cocktail glass with absinthe. Stir over ice a little longer than usual (we are looking for 25 to 30 ml dilution) and strain into the glass. Squeeze the twist over the drink, then discard.

gaz sez: *Finally someone is taking pisco to the next level. Nicely done, Anthony. These ingredients work together like a well-rehearsed Flash-Mob!*

Gondolier

Alex Malec, Ox and Stone, Rochester, NY, USA

Alex says: "This cocktail was inspired by the herbal nature Italy. The effervescence promotes the crisp nature of Italian produce. The tequila pays homage to the bar that I now call home, that allows me to explore my bartending creativity and that helps promote my skills. The drink, overall, encompasses the variety of love that my girlfriend and I experienced while visiting Italy on the most romantic trip of our lives."

2 sage leaves
1 thyme sprig
15 ml (.5 oz) fresh lemon juice
15 ml (.5 oz) simple syrup
45 ml (1.5 oz) Espolòn blanco tequila
15 ml (.5 oz) yellow Chartreuse
Ginger beer
1 curled cucumber slice, as garnish
1 thyme sprig, as garnish

Muddle the sage and thyme with lemon juice and simple syrup in a mixing glass. Add ice and the remaining ingredients. Shake and strain over ice into old-fashioned glass. Top with ginger beer and add the garnishes.

gaz sez: *Here's a perfect drink for springtime, a great quaff by the ocean in August, a fabulous cocktail to sip as the leaves turn, and it goes down pretty well in a snowstorm, too. Try it. You'll like it.*

Green Dream

Olivia Hu, Sunrise/Sunset, Brooklyn, NY, USA

Olivia says: "A refreshing drink crafted for warm weather, the cucumber juice complements the sweetness of the Mastiha well. The recipe doesn't require added sugar such as simple syrup because Mastiha is made from tree sap from the Chios islands in Greece. The ginger juice adds an extra subtle spice. A popular choice amongst the clientele, we at Sunrise/Sunset consider the Green Dream a winner."

45 ml (1.5 oz) Roots Mastiha Sweet Liquor
30 ml (1 oz) Monopolowa Vienna dry gin
60 ml (2 oz) fresh cucumber juice*
15 ml (.5 oz) fresh lemon juice
7.5 ml (.25 oz) fresh ginger juice*
Seltzer
1 cucumber wheel, as garnish
1 thyme sprig, as garnish

Shake over ice and strain into a collins glass over fresh ice. Top with seltzer and add the garnishes. Serve with 2 collins straws.

*We have a power juicer in house that we use to create the cucumber and ginger juice. Remove the skin on the ginger before juicing, but leave the cucumber unpeeled. The skin of the cucumber gives the cocktail a luminescent green color with the seltzer water.

gaz sez: *First we must look at Roots Mastiha Sweet Liquor which is actually a liqueur, not a liquor at all, and it's a pretty strange bird no matter how you look at it, but boy oh boy, it's very distinctive, indeed. I sampled Mastiha for the very first time at* *the 2015 Berlin Bar Conference, and I was really excited to see it in this drink. The Green Dream is a fabulous quaff, and if you're a gin-freak you'll be forgiven for using a little less Mastiha and a little more Mother's Ruin in this baby. Both ways work well.*

Gringo Negroni

Roberto Giudici, Fluffer Bar, Milan, Italy

Roberto says: "I've created this drink for a usual customer who wanted a twist on a Negroni with a Mexican hint. I was thinking a little bit outside the box: the "structure" of the cocktail was the same, one part for each ingredient, but each one was changed: I've replaced Campari with Spitz, an Italian gentian spirit made near Maggiore lake; the sweet red vermouth was replaced with an Italian white vermouth with citrus notes, and instead of gin I've used Del Maguey Vida, an Espadin mezcal with a complex smoky taste in mouth and in nose too. The drink was a little bit flat so I've tried to combine some bitters together. Cinchona, oranges, chocolate, every kind of ingredient that I thought could work together and with the cocktail too…I blended them to reach a standardized balance, et voilà. Enjoy!"

30 ml (1 oz) Del Maguey Vida mezcal

30 ml (1 oz) Spitz Genziana Rossi d'Angera

30 ml (1 oz) Vermouth del Professore Bianco

3 dashes Chocolate Combo Bitters*

1 orange half-wheel, as garnish

1 lemon twist, as garnish

Stir over ice and strain into a chilled tumbler over fresh ice. Add the garnishes, squeezing the twist over the drink.

*Chocolate Combo Bitters: Blend 1 part Bob's chocolate bitters, 1 part Bitter Truth Xocolatl Mole bitters, 2 parts Bitter Truth orange bitters, and 1 part Angostura bitters.

gaz sez: *Well this one was truly a pain in the ass to put together. Getting a bottle of Spitz Genziana Rossi d'Angera to the USA wasn't easy, for a start, but I have my sources . . . It was well worth the effort. One of the best Negroni variations I ever did taste. Nice one.*

Gutter Garden

Chris Stanley, Catherine Lombardi, New Brunswick, New Jersey, USA.

Chris says: "When devising this cocktail for spring season I wanted to put forth a bitter cocktail with the potential for a wide appeal.

"In addition to being a great standalone amaro, I have found Braulio to have a good affinity for tropical fruits, so passionfruit seemed a good match. A split base of this with soft genever, a little reinforcement of floral notes from chamomile, and the astringency of dandelion and burdock make for a pleasant, refreshingly herbaceous cocktail.

"In the end, balance really is the key—not taking any one element of flavor too far makes for the best combination. Not too potent either so it makes for a good aperitif.

"As for the name, I reasoned that the majority of the botanicals used in making the spirits, bitters, etc. are largely regarded as weeds or wild plants which are not purposefully cultivated."

22.5 ml (.75 oz) Braulio Amaro Alpino
22.5 ml (.75 oz) Boomsma Oude genever
22.5 ml (.75 oz) fresh lemon juice
15 ml (.5 oz) Chamomile Syrup*
15 ml (.5 oz) Passionfruit Syrup**
3 dashes Dr. Adam Elmegirab's Dandelion & Burdock bitters

Shake over ice and fine-strain into a chilled cocktail glass.

*Chamomile Syrup: Combine 480 ml (2 cups) boiling water, 500 g (2.5 cups) white sugar, and 14 g (.5 oz) dried chamomile flowers in a container and agitate until sugar is dissolved. Infuse for 24 hours; fine-strain.

**Passionfruit Syrup: Combine 480 ml (2 cups) passionfruit juice , 120 ml (4 oz) water, 250 g (1.25 cups) white sugar, and 200 g (1 cup) turbinado sugar and process with an immersion blender until the sugars are dissolved. Fine-strain twice.

gaz sez: *Pain in the Aristotle to make. Delightful to drink. The play between the genever and the Braulio in this drink is pretty stunning, and they form the backbone of bad guys who are willing to let the sweet kids (chamomile and passionfruit syrups) join in their reindeer games. Result: a shoot-out that never ends.*

Havana Daydreaming

Tony Gurdian, Imperial, Portland, OR, USA

Tony says: "My approach to cocktail creation is based on the cuisine of a given region. Lately I've been inspired by Cuba and Cuban cuisine and realized that it reminded me of the key ingredients of Calisaya. Inspired by an old Italian amaro recipe, Calisaya liqueur is an inimitable herbal liqueur that allows you to add to a sour/sweet combo without overpowering your cocktail. In terms of Cuban cuisine, I incorporated fresh bay leaf, fresh oregano, and acidic oranges in the spice syrup. I wanted to create a complex drink that was easy to make. The syrups can be made in advance so that the drink itself is quick and easy to make when ordered."

30 ml (1 oz) dry white Cuban rum (or any dry white rum)

22.5 ml (.75 oz) Calisaya

22.5 ml (.75 oz) Lime Acid Orange*

15 ml (.5 oz) Cuban Spice Syrup**

2 fresh bay leaves, as garnish

Shake over ice and double-strain into a chilled cocktail glass. Use a clip to add the garnish.

*Lime Acid Orange: This is a way to boost orange juice to the acid level of lime; cut the recipe in half or in quarters depending on how much Lime Acid Orange you need. Combine 1 L (1 qt) freshly squeezed orange juice, 32 g (1.18 oz) citric acid, and 20 g (.66 oz) malic acid. Mix with a stick blender until dissolved.

**Cuban Spice Syrup: Combine 650 ml (2.75 cups) water, 10 g (2 tsp) fresh oregano, 5 g (1 tsp) fresh bay leaves, 5 g (1 tsp) cracked and crushed black peppercorns, and 2.5 g (.5 tsp) cracked and crushed cumin seeds in a small pot and simmer on stove for 10 minutes. Strain out solids with a fine strainer and coffee filter. For every 500 ml of strained mixture, add 500 g (2 cups) sugar. Mix in a blender or stir until dissolved.

gaz sez: *God is good. This recipe landed in my in-box just one day before a bottle of Calisaya appeared on my doorstep. She's a thoughtful sort of a God, I think, but not thoughtful enough to send me pre-made Cuban Spice Syrup or Lime Acid Orange. The work was a bit of a slog, but the reward made everything worthwhile. This is one darned good drink.*

Heart's Filthy Lesson

Nick Dean, Forte the Restaurant, Jamestown, NY, USA

Nick says: "This cocktail came about after searching the web for David Bowie drinks in the days after his passing… And then wanting to make something all my own!

"I started with pomegranate vodka and Domaine de Canton because it was important to me that the drink be clear-ish, in order for the Peychaud's to stand out on top of the drink like the eye makeup on the cover of Aladdin Sane.

"After a few false starts with ginger beer and a number of liqueurs, I lucked into this combination of pomegranate, ginger, lime juice and Strega — which ended up wonderfully sweet, tart and somewhat prickly (for lack of a better word). The mint and juniper and other elements of the Strega make for a long, clean finish while also adding a certain hard-to-describe element throughout. It really unites all the other ingredients, but also blends into the background more than I initially thought it would have.

"And the Peychaud's is just the glam-tastic icing on the cake."

45 ml (1.5 oz) pomegranate vodka (gaz sez: I used Pearl Pomegranate Vodka)
15 ml (.5 oz) Strega
15 ml (.5 oz) Domaine de Canton French ginger liqueur
15 ml (.5 oz) fresh lime juice
1 dash simple syrup

2 dashes orange bitters
2 dashes Peychaud's bitters, as garnish
1 lime twist, as garnish
Shake over ice and strain into a chilled cocktail glass or coupe. Add the garnishes.

gaz sez: *Like a stream of unconnected thoughts, this baby comes across like Life on Mars, hopping from one flavor to another with no discernible reason. Nice one. RIP David Bowie. You will always be a hero of mine.*

Hidden Dragon

Kris Baljak, Clement in the Peninsula Hotel, New York, NY, USA

Kris says: "When we tasted HKB we thought it had some anise notes that would blend harmoniously with absinthe, so we tried them out and it was a good start. I added Midori to give color and a touch of sweetness. When I added the lemon and egg white initially, the cocktail became too sweet and lost some of its edge. Then I came up with the idea of separating the lemon and egg white by floating the foam on top. This way, when you sip the Hidden Dragon, the edge is there but it slightly calmed with the lemon and egg foam. In terms of the name, it's an homage to Bruce Lee. He broke racial barriers."

Foam Foundation:
30 ml (1 oz) fresh lemon juice
6 dashes Lemon Oleo-Saccharum*
3 egg whites
30 ml (1 oz) simple syrup

37.5 ml (1.25 oz) HKB baijiu
22.5 ml (.75 oz) Jade 1901 Absinthe Supérieure
15 ml (.5 oz) Midori liqueur
22.5 ml (.75 oz) fresh lemon juice
6 dashes Lemon Oleo-Saccharum*
3 viola flowers, as garnish

Combine the Foam Foundation ingredients in an N2O-charged ISI canister.

Shake the remaining ingredients over ice. Lay the Foam Foundation on the bottom of a cocktail glass about 1.5 inches deep. Slowly pour the contents of the shaker down the side of the glass so the liquid lies under the foam. Add the garnish.

*Lemon Oleo-Saccharum: Peel 6 lemons, taking care to avoid the pith. Combine the peels with 100 g (.5 cup) granulated sugar and let stand for 30 minutes. Muddle the peels slightly to release more oils and let stand another hour before straining.

gaz sez: *Whatever happened to Gin and Tonics? How about Scotch and Soda? Now I have to make foams (thanks, Jamie Boudreau, Dave Arnold, et al), then I need to make Oleo-Saccharum (I won't forget this, David Wondrich), and all this has to be done before I even attempt to make the [expletive deleted] drink. Oy Vey!*

That said, I have an extreme fondness for baijiu, having first sampled it in China a few years ago, and although it sometimes bears that unmistakable eau de sweaty socks aroma, it's a very pleasant eau de sweaty socks, if you know what I mean. Acquired taste? Maybe, but it's a taste that, in my opinion, is well worth acquiring.

And to go back to the Hidden Dragon cocktail, let me just say this: It Rocks! And it's worth a trip to NYC to sample it if you don't want to fiddle with the foam or mess around with sugar and lemon zests to make something with a Latin name. Sometimes I yearn for 1973 . . .

High Society Cocktail

Verrier Maxime, Pollen Street Social, London, UK

Verrier says: "This cocktail was inspired by two classic cocktails: the Stinger—cognac and white crème de menthe in a shaker, from around 1914—and the Brandy Cocktail—brandy, white crème de menthe, and angostura in a mixing glass, garnished with a lemon peel, which appeared in Modern American Drinks by George J. Kappeler around 1900.

"The name was inspired by the eponymous 1956 movie *High Society* starring Frank Sinatra, where the Stinger cocktail appeared. So it's an homage to the Stinger and the close relation between Chivas and Frank Sinatra at this period. Cheers!"

60 ml (2 oz) Chivas 12-year-old scotch whisky
15 ml (.5 oz) white crème de menthe
1 barspoon Fernet Branca
1 small mint leaf, as garnish

Combine all the ingredients in a shaker with ice, then thrown to the empty part of the shaker. Repeat 3 to 5 times depending of the quality of the ice, then strain into a chill coupette. Use a miniature clothes peg to attach the garnish.

gaz sez: *High Society, indeed! This is a sophisticated dram that could hold its own at any posh old Gentleman's Club in London, for instance, but it would also feel at home near a cozy wood fire when friends come over to visit. The Fernet Branca brings this baby together without once interrupting the scotch or the crème de menthe. I'll be drinking more of these.*

Honey Badger

Liam Baer, Fish and Meat, Hong Kong

Liam says: "I came up with this drink on a cool fall night in NYC. A customer came in and asked for a cold variation of a hot toddy. I whipped this up using fresh rosemary and later decided to infuse it into the bourbon for better flavor incorporation."

45 ml (1.5 oz) Rosemary-Infused Bourbon* (Liam prefers Buffalo Trace)
15 ml (.5 oz) yellow Chartreuse

20 ml (.66 oz) fresh lemon juice
10 ml (.33 oz) honey syrup (2:1)
10 ml (.33 oz) Ginger Syrup**
2 dashes Fee Brothers lemon bitters
Lemon oil, as garnish
1 small rosemary sprig, as garnish

Shake over ice and double-strain into a chilled old-fashioned glass. Add the garnishes.

*Rosemary-Infused Bourbon: Combine six fresh rosemary sprigs with 750 ml bourbon. Let sit for 48 hours than strain and rebottle.

**Ginger Syrup: Combine 100 g (1/2 cup) brown sugar and 100 ml (about 1/3 cup) water in a saucepan and bring to a boil. Stir until sugar is melted and have a nice light brown simple syrup. Let cool slightly, then place the syrup and 100 g (1 cup) peeled and chopped fresh ginger into an electric blender and blend on high until you have a paste. Using a fine strainer, strain out the solids. You should have a nice smooth ginger syrup when finished. Bottle and refrigerate.

gaz sez: *This baby's all over the place, but it nestles gracefully in its sett (that's where badgers live, lest you didn't know), and the drink yields a fabulously spicy, herbal body with a wonderful hint of citrus from the lemon bitters. Nicely executed, Liam.*

Isle of Pheasants

Rick Paulger, Michael Symon's Roast, Detroit, MI, USA

Rick says: "This drink was created for a contest in which participants were required to use a minimum of 1 ounce of Licor 43 as the sugar element. I jumped at the challenge of balancing that amount of sweetness, without suffocating the liqueur, and subsequently won the day!"

30 ml (1 oz) Laird's Straight apple brandy
30 ml (1 oz) Salers Gentiane aperitif
30 ml (1 oz) Licor 43
15 ml (.5 oz) fresh lime juice

2 dashes Angostura bitters
1 lime wheel, as garnish
1 dehydrated apple slice, as garnish
Shake over ice and double-strain into a chilled cocktail glass. Add the garnish.

gaz sez: *Nice to see Licor 43 being used so darned creatively—the Salers makes for a perfect foil, and the applejack provides a sturdy backbone for the cocktail. This one works without the lime juice, too—give it a try.*

It Doesn't Take an Empire

Simon Ford, The 86 Co, New York, NY

60 ml (2 oz) Fords gin
15 ml (.5 oz) fresh lemon juice
22.5 ml (.75 oz) simple syrup

30 ml (1 oz) Martini & Rossi Sweet Vermouth Infusion*
1 dash Angostura bitters
Club soda
1 maraschino cherry, as garnish

Shake over ice and strain into a highball glass. Top with soda and add the garnish.

*Martini & Rossi Sweet Vermouth Infusion: Take a one liter or 750ml bottle of Martini & Rossi sweet vermouth and infuse it with 4 or 3 heaping tablespoons of market spice/chai tea. Let it sit for 1.5 hours. Strain and keep refrigerated.

gaz sez: *"Keep it Simple, Stupid" is not a bad catch-phrase, and although Simon managed to keep it simple with this recipe, he's far from being stupid. Lest you didn't know, Simon is one of the owners of The 86 Company that offers top-of-the-line spirits at ultra-reasonable prices, packed in bartender-friendly bottles. And he's a damned good bartender, too!*

Jasmine Limoncello

Stephen Dennison, Bistro 1860, Louisville, KY, USA

Stephen says: "So here you are fat-washing, using an essential oil. There are hundreds of these that can be introduced to spirits. They pack a lot of flavor in a small amount, so don't overdo it! You also have to be mindful—some essential oils are not fit for internal use and some are myths when it comes to internal use (cinnamon challenge, bergamot). Research their use and don't serve them if you wouldn't want to drink them.

"The prep time for this is minimal. To execute, you simply pour. Then watch people's eyes light up. This is an elegant way to end an evening. A nice, floral twist on a classic."

1 L vodka of choice

6 lemons, quartered

4 to 6 drops jasmine essential oil

1 L (1 generous quart) simple syrup (1:1)

Pour the vodka into a nonreactive container. Squeeze the lemon wedges into the vodka, and drop in the shells. Add the jasmine oil, stir briefly, and refrigerate for a week. Strain through a chinois or a double layer of moistened cheesecloth, add the simple syrup, and store in the freezer or refrigerator until service.

gaz sez: *I'm a sucker for limoncello after first tasting some at Al Forno restaurant in Providence, Rhode Island, back in the '90s, and this easy-to-make variation is just fabulous. When adding the simple syrup, I advise you to add just half of it first, then refrigerate and taste it before adding more. This way you can set the sweetness level to suit your own palate. The small amount of jasmine oil in this baby makes all the difference in the world.*

Keen-A On You

Donny Clutterbuck, Good Luck, Rochester, NY, USA

Donny says: "I've been putting damn near everything into the daiquiri build structure, and this has been one of my absolute favorites. I love the complexity that a high-proof, whiskey-like, grape- and floral-tasting cognac adds to the mix. The China China adds a bit more depth of flavor, and integrates seamlessly with the Force 53."

> 45 ml (1.5 oz) Louis Royer Force 53 VSOP cognac
> 15 ml (.5 oz) Bigallet China China
> 22.5 ml (.75 oz) fresh fine-strained lime juice
> 22.5 ml (.75 oz) demerara syrup (1:1)
> 1 lime peel, as garnish
> Shake vigorously over ice until the shaker frosts over (and maybe even then some). Double-strain into a chilled coupe and add the garnish.

gaz sez: *I'd never tried Bigallet China China before, and I found it on-line at K&L Wines. Their web site describes it thusly: "This is truly the quintessential bitter French liqueur. They start with high quality neutral spirit. Both bitter and sweet orange peels are macerated in the base spirit before being distilled. Then they do it again. Wait, then they do it one more time. Then they add more peels, spices, botanicals, etc. A small amount of sugar is used to balance the bitter and stabilize the color. This is the*

Franco-phonic answer to Amaro and it is so so good. Truly a special treat for anyone smart enough to include this in their shopping list. It can also be used as a substitute for bitter liqueurs in various cocktails, vermouth and amaro alike."

That said, then, this cocktail rocks. It's well worth investing in a bottle of Bigallet China China just to experience this baby. Trust me on this.

Killer Queen

Zachary Nelson, The Hammer Bar, Anaheim, CA, USA

Zachary says: "This was another one of those on-the-fly creations. A customer wanted something with mezcal that was spicy yet refreshing. I had been playing with Ancho Reyes/mezcal combos, and this one really hit the spot. The passionfruit syrup adds a level of unparalleled refreshment, while the chocolate-chile bitters provide just the right kind of spice to keep you coming back for more. Our bar manager, Lucie Wood, makes the passionfruit syrup and house chocolate-chile bitters."

30 ml (1 oz) Illegal Mezcal Joven
30 ml (1 oz) Ancho Reyes
22.5 ml (.75 oz) Passionfruit Syrup*
22.5 ml (.75 oz) fresh lime juice
3 dashes Ghost Chile-Cacao Bitters**
1 dried chile, as garnish

Shake over ice and double-strain into highball glass over crushed ice. Add the garnish.

*Passionfruit Syrup: Make a 2:1 simple syrup with 450 g (2 cups) granulated sugar and 240 ml (1 cup) water (hot method). When cooled, add 240 ml (1 cup) shelf-stable passionfruit juice concentrate (such as Maguary, available on Amazon or Latin grocery stores). Pour into a 750-ml bottle and store in the refrigerator.

**Ghost Chile-Cacao Bitters: Combine 240 ml (1 cup) flavorful 151-proof rum (such as Gosling's 151 or Hamilton 151 Jamaican), 1 pitted and quartered Medjool date, and 1/4 cup cacao nibs in a glass jar. Cover and allow to infuse for 7 days. Add 1/2 cinnamon stick, 1 allspice berry, and 1 teaspoon black walnut leaf. Cover and infuse for 24 hours. Strain and add 2 quartered ghost chiles (use gloves!). Infuse for 30 minutes to 1 hour (to taste). Remove the chiles, strain through a coffee filter, and bottle. Makes about 240 ml (1 cup). Alternatively you can use 2 dashes Bitter Truth Chocolate bitters plus 2 to 3 dashes Scrappy's Habanero Firewater Cocktail bitters.

gaz sez: *F***in' brilliant. I bet this drink will sell over and over again in any bar in the world. Nicely done, Zachary!*

King Louie the 4th

Anthony DeSerio, Sticks & Stones, Uncasville, CT, USA

Anthony says: "This is one of the most recent cocktails I've put together. I wanted to put a hefty twist on a Vieux Carré and the honey flavors of Monkey Shoulder were on my mind. I thought of honey and ginger. So instead of American whiskey, Cognac and sweet vermouth, I subbed these all out for a lovely gateway blended scotch, ginger cognac, and port cut with Lillet. The chocolate bitters pull all the flavors together. This silky tannic twist gets its name from my friend's favorite monkey, King Louie [from Disney's 1967 adaptation of The Jungle Book], and the French Quarter of NOLA where the origins of this cocktail spun off from."

30 ml (1 oz) Monkey Shoulder scotch whisky
22.5 ml (.75 oz) Domaine de Canton French ginger liqueur
15 ml (.5 oz) Taylor Fladgate 10 year old tawny port
15 ml (.5 oz) Lillet Rouge
1 teaspoon Bénédictine
4 to 5 drops chocolate mole bitters
1 skewered maraschino cherry, as garnish
Stir over ice and strain into a chilled coupe. Add the garnish.

gaz sez: *I featured this one on scotchwhisky.com in March, 2016, and told Anthony that, since he already had one drink in this year's book, I couldn't* *include this one too. Then I tasted it again and said screw it! This drink is far too good to not list in 101BNC. Don't just trust me on this. Try it. You won't regret it. Honest.*

Kirkwall Kelpie

Phil Barlow, The Seamstress, New York, NY, USA

Phil says: "About the drink itself, the brief was to create a cocktail containing Highland Park Dark Origins and maple syrup . . . [and] I thought the addition of saline solution would cut through the sweetness and dry the cocktail out.

"The salt water element led me to think of coastal stories and myths. Kirkwall is the coastal town where Highland Park is made, and the kelpie is a Scottish water spirit which assumes the appearance of a horse when on land. It is a mythical story which would be told to children to keep them away from water. It was said that if you touched a kelpie you would become stuck to it and it would then drag you into the water and drown you. A dark story to match the Dark Origins.

"Recently, there have been two statues erected in my home town of Falkirk of the Kelpies, which I suppose is where the thinking came from."

45 ml (1.5 oz) Highland Park Dark Origins scotch whisky

22.5 ml (.75 oz) oloroso or amontillado sherry*

7.5 ml (.25 oz) maple syrup

2 dashes chocolate bitters

3 drops saline solution (5:1)

Baby's breath, as garnish

Stir over ice and strain into a small old-fashioned glass. Add the garnish.

*This drink works well with both oloroso and amontillado sherries, though the creator favors the drier bottling and gaz likes the oloroso version best. Try 'em both, why doncha?

gaz sez: *This drink came to me by way of perhaps the best press kit I've ever seen. It contained every ingredient in the drink, a very handsome mixing glass, a strainer, and a barspoon. There was a nifty little booklet that told me a little about the drink, about*

Phil Barlow, and of course, about Highland Park Dark Origins scotch. I made the cocktail within ten minutes of opening the package. It's just fabulous.

There was no baby's breath in the press kit since, of course, there was a good chance it wouldn't have survived the trip, so I had to go without this delightful garnish when I first sampled the drink. An orange twist works well if you're in the same boat.

Lime in the Coconut

Andrew Aoun, TAPS Fish House & Brewery, Brea, CA, USA

Andrew says: "We really want to show people that a piña colada was not something that comes out of a can or plastic bottle. This was a slightly modified version with a lot of character that made the drink approachable but interesting. We also do it in a liquid nitrogen version....."

45 ml (1.5 oz) Coruba coconut rum
15 ml (.5 oz) SelvaRey Cacao rum
22.5 ml (.75 oz) Giffard orgeat syrup
22.5 ml (.75 oz) fresh lime juice
22.5 ml (.75 oz) fresh pineapple juice
22.5 ml (.75 oz) heavy cream
1 lime wheel, as garnish
Grated nutmeg, as garnish
Pineapple leaves, as garnish

Shake over ice and strain into a chilled collins glass. Fill with crushed ice and add the garnishes.

gaz sez: *I must admit that I paper-judged this and found it not to be of my liking, but there was something about it that made me keep going back and looking at the recipe again over and over. Eventually I decided to try the damned thing. It's absolutely marvelous. Well done, Andrew!*

Lion & Rose

Samuel Tripet, Lily Blacks, Melbourne, Victoria, Australia

Samuel says: "This drink was inspired by growing up with idolistic masculine and feminine influences. Having a balance of the two was very important to me. The Lion & Rose cocktail represents harmony between two great forces."

25 ml (.8 oz) Lagavulin 16 year old scotch whisky
25 ml (.8 oz) Amaro Montenegro

25 ml (.8 oz) Dolin dry vermouth
1 lemon twist, as garnish
Stir over ice and strain into a chilled cocktail glass. Add the garnish.

gaz sez: *Kindly excuse a little blasphemy here: Jesus Christ Almighty, this is one incredibly fabulous drink. I could sip on these all night. As long as I sipped them slowly, of course, and that's near as damn it impossible.*

Little Dragon

Humberto Marques, CURFEW, Copenhagen, Denmark

Humberto says: "A cocktail created for the summer menu, but this cocktail could be sipped all year. A perfect pairing between mango, green tea, and dry sherry makes a perfect match with Tanqueray gin along with tarragon to temper the coolness between all of the ingredients. As John Evelyn says of tarragon: 'Tis highly cordial and friend to the head, heart and liver.' A little dragon it is!"

50 ml (1.7 oz) Tanqueray gin
50 ml (1.7 oz) mango puree
20 ml (.66 oz) dry sherry
20 ml (.66 oz) fresh lemon juice
15 ml (.5 oz) honey
1 pinch green tea powder (matcha)
1 tarragon sprig, as garnish
Shake over ice and strain into an ice-filled goblet. Add the garnish.

gaz sez: *It's hard to tell where the tail to the dragon ends in this drink—it's the longest short cocktail I ever did sip. And it's absolutely fabulous. Humberto seems to know what he's doing, I think!*

Loop

Andreas Sanidiotis, Lost + Found Drinkery, Nicosia, Cyprus

60 ml (2 oz) Bacardi Superior rum
15 ml (.5 oz) fresh lemon juice
20 ml (.66 oz) Strawberry Oleo Saccharum*
3 basil leaves
2 dashes balsamic vinegar
3 dashes green Chartreuse
1 fresh basil sprig, as garnish

Shake over ice and fine-strain into a collins glass. Top with crushed ice and add the garnish.

*Strawberry Oleo Saccharum: Muddle 200 g (1 cup) caster or superfine sugar, 150 g (about 1 cup) fresh stemmed strawberries, and the peel from 1 lemon in a bowl. Cover and let it sit overnight, until sugar is dissolved.

gaz sez: *There was something about the combination of Chartreuse and balsamic vinegar that made me need to test this drink, and it's a pretty weird wedding, for sure, but it does work, and this drink is more than worthy of a place in this collection. And the strawberry oleo saccharum is pretty darned good, too!*

M&M´s

Philipp M. Ernst, Bar 67, Ischgl, Tirol, Austria

Philipp says: "Dear Gaz! Greetings from Austria! Do you remember the Retro, Disco, Future Challenge at Cape Town - you told me, I should send the Recipe - you would have my Drink for your Book 101 Best New Drinks - this was one of my greatest moments at World Class! Thank you!"

45 ml (1.5 oz) Tanqueray No. TEN
30 ml (1 oz) Carpano Antica Formula
2 dashes chocolate bitters
1 dash orange bitters

Ginger Beer Foam*

M&M´s by side

Stir over ice and strain into a chilled glass. Top with Ginger Beer Foam and serve with some M&M´s as food pairing.

*Ginger Beer Foam: Combine 250 ml (8 oz) Ginger Beer and 2 g (.5 teaspoon) lecithin and mix with an immersion blender to create foam.

gaz sez: *I sampled this drink in South Africa during the 2015 finals of Diageo's World Class Bartender competition. It's just fabulous. My kind of session drink.*

Magic Julep

Giuseppe González, Suffolk Arms, New York, NY

8 to 10 fresh mint leaves

30 ml (1 oz) simple syrup

30 ml (1 oz) Fernet Branca

30 ml (1 oz) Angostura bitters

1 fresh mint sprig, as garnish

Muddle the mint leaves in the simple syrup in the bottom of a Julep cup. Add crushed ice and the remaining ingredients. Stir well, add more crushed ice to form a cone on top of the drink, and add the garnish.

gaz sez: *In April, 2016, I was in Manhattan to conduct a Mindful Bartender presentation at a midtown hotel, so I figured I'd look at Giuseppe González' new joint, Suffolk Arms, to see if it was really as fabulous as everyone had been telling me. It was. It was more than that.*

I spent a delightful couple of hours in this joint, and my drink of choice was Giuseppe's Magic Julep. It's a delightful quaff, and Giuseppe is a delightful chap, too. Well done, Brother. You constantly take us to new heights, and amazingly, you've managed to open a 5-star craft cocktail bar that feels like a neighborhood hang-out.

Mama Cass

Yuval Soffer, Gatsby, Jerusalem, Israel

Yuval says: "This drink is now two years old. It's doing really well in a lot of bars in Tel Aviv so I thought I should share the love."

Pernod, as rinse
1 egg white
22.5 ml (.75 oz) honey syrup (3:1)
22.5 ml (.75 oz) fresh lemon juice
30 ml (1 oz) London dry gin
30 ml (1 oz) Becherovka
Peychaud's bitters, as garnish
1 star anise pod, as garnish

Rinse a double old-fashioned glass with Pernod and add ice. Shake all ingredients vigorously, then strain into another shaker and shake again without ice. Double-strain into the glass and add the garnishes.

gaz sez: *I'm a bit of an anise freak, so this was a natch for me, and I must say that gin and Becherovka tango tightly in the Mama Cass cocktail. The Peychaud's as an aromatic garnish, here, though, really adds the crown to the drink and makes it stand head and tails above the rest of the crowd.*

Maman Brigitte

Tristan Simon, A La Française, Paris, France

Tristan says: "This recipe came across my mind while doing research on the next cocktail menu for the bar. I was considering the French rhum agricole part, and wondering how I could balance this typical French spirit with some traditional cocktail recipes. At some point I got to the Brandy Alexander, with is a personal favorite... Then for some reason I considered twisting it with some classic tiki aromatics. Maman Brigitte was born!

"As for the name, you may wonder. I first considered calling it 'Baron Samedi,' for the Voodoo Iwa (god) of death and resurrection. Then I considered it was kind of a common name. With further research it appeared the guy had a wife, 'Maman Brigitte,' Iwa of death (too) and also of curing ulcers (an always useful skill!).

"I then ended up with a tiki twist on the Brandy Alexander, based on uncommonly used French rhum, named after a Voodoo goddess of death and curing ulcers. It was a complete go!"

30 ml (1 oz) St James Rum Agricole Imperial Blanc
20 ml (.66 oz) St James Rum Agricole Royal Ambre
10 ml (.33 oz) Marie Brizard Chocolat Royal liqueur
10 ml (.33 oz) Monin falernum syrup
20 ml (.66 oz) heavy cream
10 ml (.33 oz) coconut cream
Grated nutmeg, as garnish

Shake vigorously over ice (in a Japanese-style shaker, if available). Double-strain into a chilled cocktail glass and add the garnish. Drink, santé!

gaz sez: *I'll take 5 of these after dinner, please. Every day of the week . . .*

Marmalade Duke

Jonathan Downs, Abode Canterbury Champagne Bar, Canterbury, Kent, UK

Jonathan says: "The Marmalade Duke is a rich and decadent cocktail combining the rich bittersweet flavour of Chase Marmalade vodka, with the smooth, nuttiness of Briottet Crème de Châtaigne liqueur, the sweetness of Monin chocolate syrup and the bitterness of fresh espresso coffee. Once shaken together it is served with a creamy layer of Baileys at the bottom of the glass. The cocktail is then garnished with an orange slice that has been soaked in sugar syrup and then dried out in an oven, which adds a great contrast to the cocktail. A perfect well balanced serve for after dinner, either paired with a dessert or petit fours, or simply for whenever the mood takes you.

"The Marmalade Duke is an evolution of the popular Espresso Martini, but with a richer, fuller and more complex finish. The Chase Marmalade vodka is the base spirit of the cocktail. Its sweetness and huge flavor, thanks to the Seville oranges helps to cut through the bitterness of the fresh espresso coffee which is rounded with the chocolate syrup. Added to this is the chestnut liqueur which is made from a maceration of chestnuts from the Ardèche department in France adding more depth to the cocktail and complements the Seville orange, coffee and chocolate flavours. The Irish liqueur gives the cocktail a creamy, more luxurious finish and adds more complexity to the taste on the palate.

"The layering technique is a bit of a showmanship, for once the drink has settled and you pour the Baileys down a barspoon in the middle of the drink it settles fairly easily and amazes the viewer, and I found this method slightly easier than layering the Baileys first. The top layer of the drink is the foam created from shaking the cocktail.

"I came up with the drink as an alternative version of the Espresso Martini, partly in thanks to a conversation I had with a guest at my bar who couldn't decide between an Espresso Martini or a Baileys for after their meal. The choice of the different range of flavours was for me wanting to create a dessert in a cocktail, having more depth in taste with the orange, chestnut, coffee and chocolate and the rounded off with the creamy Baileys liqueur, which helps to lengthen the complex finish on the palate."

40 ml (1.35 oz) Chase Marmalade vodka

25 ml (.8 oz) espresso shot

20 ml (.66 oz) Briottet Crème de Châtaigne liqueur

10 ml (.33 oz) Monin chocolate syrup

20 ml (.66 oz) Baileys

1 Candied Dried Orange Slice*, as garnish

Shake the first four ingredients over ice and strain into a chilled coupe. Once the cocktail has settled, use a barspoon to layer the Baileys at the bottom of the glass. Add the garnish.

*Candied Dried Orange Slice: Cut an orange into thin slices and soak overnight in sugar syrup. Drain and place on a baking tray lined with a nonstick baking mat. Transfer to a 200°F oven and bake until the flesh of the orange is translucent and the peel is dry, roughly 2.5 hours.

gaz sez: *Often we like to think that we're too sophisticated to enjoy sweet concoctions, but we also know deep down that that's not strictly true—they are just more like secret lovers than out-in-the-open affairs, and let's face it, they sell like crazy. This beauty is way more complex than most drinks of its ilk, and the flavors go together astonishingly well. Promise.*

Mezcalero

David A. Roth, Cask Bar & Kitchen, New York, NY, USA

David says: "Meet the Mezcalero. This is a drink of mine that I am very proud of. The inspiration comes from the Far East, China to be exact. My inspiration was General Tso's chicken. I was enjoying a plate of delicious, crispy, orange chicken. The sauce was so good and I thought, "Why can't cocktails taste like this?" So I set out to make a delicious orange-flavored drink that had layers of flavor and would appeal to men and women. I had recently noticed that Cointreau was bottled at 80 proof and there were no cocktails that I knew of that used it as a base spirit. Next, I added a little Domaine de Canton because the ginger really complemented the orange liqueur and they were both French, they should get along well. Fresh lemon juice was added to brighten and grapefruit bitters for more citrus notes and complexity. Mezcal was added to give another dimension of flavor and aroma. An earthiness that took the drink to another level and after that, it could only be named the Mezcalero. I have to thank my friends and co-workers for their suggestions on the year-long evolution of this drink. Dan G., Josh P. and Naren Y.—this drink is amazing because of your support. Hope you like the Mezcalero as much as I do. Not bad for something that started with a mouthful of crispy, orange chicken. Cheers!"

45 ml (1.5 oz) Cointreau (Combier works well too)
15 ml (.50 oz) Domaine de Canton
15 ml (.50 oz) Vida Mezcal
22.5 ml (.75 oz) fresh lemon juice
2 dashes grapefruit bitters (Fee Brothers works well)
1 grapefruit twist, as garnish
Mezcal "Smoke"*, as garnish

Shake vigorously over ice for 10 seconds. Double-strain into a chilled cocktail glass or coupe. Squeeze the twist over the drink, then kiss the rim as well and add as garnish. Mist the Mezcal "Smoke" over the Mezcalero to let the guests know that something juicy, smoky and delicious is coming their way.

*Mezcal "Smoke" is simply Vida Mezcal in an atomizer. Hold a few inches up and away from the drink. Pump the atomizer once or twice at the most towards the drink and watch as the smoky mist falls on top of the glass.

gaz sez: *I've been wondering how long it would take before someone started created cocktails based on Chinese food, and David just went and dun it. Nice one, sir! And I loved hearing how it all came together—this is a brill drink, indeed.*

MiAmor

Angelika Larkina, EBA Training Center, Tallinn, Harjumaa, Estonia

Angelika says: "MiAmor is my Bacardi Legacy Cocktail Competition 2016 Baltic finalist. The inspiration for this cocktail was the love, like the name already refers.

"Love is the most powerful feeling in the world. There is never a time or place for true love. It happens accidentally, in a heartbeat, in a single flashing, throbbing moment.

"The first sip of the cocktail is pink like the first time you saw your beloved one with air full of strawberry and raspberry aromas. Berries are followed by the apricots that give strong posture and help you to get to know each other. Smokiness and floral touch that comes from muscovado sugar helps you to fly and do everything for beloved one.

"And then comes passion… passion that cannot be tamed like Bacardi, that could not be tamed by floods, earthquakes, fires! Passion for each other! Try and feel the love!"

50 ml (1.7 oz) Bacardi Carta Oro rum
20 ml (.66 oz) Martini & Rossi Rosato vermouth
1 barspoon apricot brandy
2 barspoons dark muscovado sugar syrup (2:1)
2 dashes orange bitters
1 orange twist, as garnish
Stir over ice and strain into a chilled coupette. Add the garnish.

gaz sez: *Me Amour MiAmor. It's the kind of love that lingers on the breath reminding you of so many wonderful moments in life. It's pretty much an eternal love, I think.*

Mime's Well

Chris Grøtvedt, THE THIEF, Oslo, Norway

15 ml (.5 oz) Lagavulin 16 Year Old single malt scotch whisky, as a rinse

45 ml (1.5 oz) Buffalo Trace bourbon

15 ml (.5 oz) Coffee-Infused Carpano Antica Formula*

10 ml (.33 oz) Smoked Pedro Ximénez Sherry Reduction**

2 barspoons Fernet Branca

1 dash Angostura bitters

1 dash chocolate bitters

1 orange twist, as garnish

Rinse a chilled (preferably from the freezer) coupette with the scotch. Add a chunk of hand-carved ice to the glass.

Stir the remaining ingredients over ice. Strain into the coupette and add the garnish.

*Coffee-Infused Carpano Antica Formula: Combine 1 cup coffee beans and 750 ml vermouth. Let stand at room temperature for 4 hours before straining and rebottling.

**Smoked Pedro Ximénez Sherry Reduction: Combine half a bottle of good PX with 200 ml (a little over .75 cup) of Lagavulin 16 Year Old single malt scotch over medium heat. Add 150 g (.75 cup) sugar and let it simmer for around 20 minutes. Take it off and let it chill. Store in the refrigerator.

gaz sez: *This baby is just incredible. Takes a bit of work to put it together, but it's an ideal drink for fans of smoke, coffee, vanilla, you name it—Mime's Well Ends Well, too!*

Mumbaiced Tea

Alfonso del Portillo, The Anthologist, London, UK

Alfonso says: "This is the cocktail that I was presenting in the Retro, Disco, Future challenge in the World Class in South Africa, this being the one that I made for you, the Disco one. To refresh your memory I am the Spanish guy who was representing India in World Class, and as you told me that you liked my drink, I guess I will give it a try and send it to you.

The idea for this drink came as it is one of the most iconic Disco drinks, as it is one of the most ordered drinks still in India."

20 ml (.66 oz) Tanqueray No. TEN
20 ml (.66 oz) Grand Marnier
20 ml (.66 oz) Don Julio blanco tequila
25 ml (.8 oz) Grapefruit Shrub*

20 ml (.66 oz) Coca Cola & Black Tea Syrup**

Club soda

Shake hard over ice, but not for too long, as we don't want much dilution in our drink. Fine-strain into a small crystal bowl and top off with club soda.

*Grapefruit Shrub: Zest and juice 2 large grapefruits. Mix the zest with 150 g (3/4 cup) refined sugar in a bowl. Muddle it and cover it with plastic film for an hour. This way the sugar will get the aromas of the zest. Discard the zest and blend the resultant sugar with 180 ml (3/4 cup) apple cider vinegar and the grapefruit juice. Let it sit into an airtight jar for three days and strain it through a cloth.

**Coca Cola & Black Tea Syrup: Mix equal parts of Coke and black tea (brewed with 1 teaspoon for every 100 ml [3.3 oz] of water). Make a syrup using 2 parts sugar to 1 part of the resultant liquid.

gaz sez: *I tasted this one in South Africa this year at the finals of Diageo's World Class Bartender competition. I was helping judge the "Retro/Disco/Future" challenge with Ueno-San and Tim Phillips, that diminutive chappie from Down Under, and this little number, Alfonso's Disco drink, fair blew me away. It's a pain in the ass to make, but the results are a thing of great beauty.*

A Murder of Goth Chicks

Sean Enright, Tiki Lounge, Pittsburgh, PA

Sean says: "This drink was originally created for a whiskey event as I had just started reading Beachbum Berry's tiki guides. I wanted to create a non-typical tiki drink and I liked the balance of sweet and bitter in this cocktail. The name comes from 'what would you call a group of goth girls?' which the answer is obviously 'a murder'... like a murder of crows."

22.5 ml (.75 oz) Averna amaro

45 ml (1.5 oz) bourbon

22.5 ml (.75 oz) Don's Mix*

7.5 ml (.25 oz) orgeat syrup

6 dashes Bittermens Elemakule Tiki bitters

Guinness, as float

Pour amaro into a rocks glass. Carefully add one large ice cube so as not to disturb the amaro.

Shake over ice and double-strain slowly over the ice cube. Float the Guinness on top with spigot as close to the ice cube as possible.

*Don's Mix: This recipe is from Don the Beachcomber: Combine two parts fresh grapefruit juice with 1 part cinnamon simple syrup. Store in an airtight container in the refrigerator until ready to use. (To make cinnamon syrup, combine 200 g (1 cup) sugar, 240 ml (1 cup) water, and a 2-inch piece of cinnamon bark in a saucepan. Set over low heat for 5 minutes. Let stand overnight and then strain. Store in an airtight container in the refrigerator until ready to use.)

gaz sez: *Too bloody weird not to try, right? This one is just astonishing. 'Nuf said.*

Negroni Chinato

Matteo Schianchi, Prospero, Reggio Emilia, Italy

Matteo says: "A twist on a classic of the legendary Negroni, this uses China Bisleri instead of Campari and two dashes of grapefruit bitters to give more freshness to my drink."

40 ml (1.35 oz) Martini & Rossi Rosso vermouth
35 ml (1.17 oz) Oxley gin
20 ml (.66 oz) Bisleri Ferro-China liqueur
2 dashes Fee Brothers grapefruit bitters
1 lemon twist, as garnish
Stir over ice and strain in a chilled cocktail glass. Add the garnish.

gaz sez: *China Bisleri isn't widely available, I'm afraid, but a good bartender friend in Italy tested this recipe for me, and she just raved about the drink, saying that the grapefruit bitters were the finishing touch that made this cocktail stand very tall indeed, so I'm including it in this year's 101BNC. Can't wait to get to Italy to try it for myself!*

New Fashioned

Sonny De Lido, Pizza East Shoreditch, London, England, UK

Sonny says: "Many ladies don't like Old-Fashioneds so I made one for them. I replaced the sugar cube with a barspoon of maraschino and a hint of blackberries!"

40 ml (1.35 oz) Woodford Reserve bourbon
15 ml (.5 oz) crème de mûre
5 ml (.16 oz or 1 teaspoon) maraschino liqueur
2 drops Angostura bitters
1 lemon twist, as garnish
Stir over ice in an old-fashioned glass and add the garnish.

gaz sez: *Sonny says that he created the New Fashioned for the ladies, and if that's the case I've been using the wrong restroom all my life. This drink suits me down to the ground. Nice one, Sonny!*

Not Too Sloe

Francesco Lombardi, The Walrus Room, London, England, UK

Francesco says: "I wanted to create a softer alternative to a classic Negroni, and doesn't scare the ladies off! Soften it up with Aperol instead of Campari, and add a British touch with the sloe gin (Plymouth is my choice—it's creamy and has a very fruity aftertaste). The pink grapefruit juice adds the freshness and a slightly bitter taste to complement the Aperol. The cherry bitters give a nice aroma. Makes a great brunch aperitif or early evening drink, and an easy start for all those Negroni lovers out there like me."

25 ml (.8 oz) Plymouth sloe gin
25 ml (.8 oz) London dry gin
15 ml (.5 oz) Aperol
15 ml (.5 oz) Carpano Antica Formula
10 ml (.33 oz) fresh pink grapefruit juice
2 dashes cherry bitters
1 Amarena cherry, as garnish
1 orange twist, as garnish
Stir over ice and strain into a chilled coupe. Add the garnishes.

gaz sez: *Sloe gin does a fabulous job in this cocktail. It's one of those "why didn't I think of that" ingredients. And the cherry bitters (I used Fee Brothers) add a fabulous dimension to the drink. Not Too Sloe should be consumed quickly!*

Old Buccaneer

Ivan Di Giovanni, The Walrus Room, London, England, UK

Ivan says: "The idea of this drink came to me thanks to my father. He does, indeed, look like a pirate and, because of his look and his love for anisette I have decided to blend together Jamaican rum with Absinthe.

"I have chosen Jamaican rum for its richness and aroma. I find them full and pungent and slightly sweeter than other rums.

"I have also chosen Jamaican rum for the location of the island itself in the heart of the Caribbean Sea from where the term 'buccaneer' came from. In facts, Buccaneers were pirates that used to attack Spanish ships in the heart of the Caribbean Sea.

"I love this drink!" Ivan Di Giovanni

50 ml (1.7 oz) Jamaican rum

10 ml (.33 oz) Absinthe

20 ml (.66 oz) fresh lime juice

10 ml (.33 oz) simple syrup

3 dashes Dr. Adam Elmegirab's Orinoco bitters

1 mint sprig, as garnish

Grated dark chocolate, as garnish

Shake over ice and fine-strain into a rocks glass over an ice block. Add the garnishes.

]**gaz sez:** *I love this drink, too, Ivan, and I chose to include it in this batch of 101BNC because of the fine job you did in balancing the ingredients—the Absinthe is evident, but not overpowering, and the Orinoco bitters pull the whole thing together pretty elegantly. Yo Ho Ho!*

Old Fashioned Holiday

Michael Gatlin, Evo, Portland, ME, USA

Michael says: "I was asked by the owners of Evo to make some festive drinks for the Christmas season. This one was hands-down everyone's favorite. The nutmeg and cinnamon mix well with the autumn spices of the Averna. So this drink is now on our winter menu."

60 ml (2 oz) Nutmeg-Infused Old Overholt Rye*

15 ml (.5 oz) Averna amaro

15 ml (.5 oz) Cinnamon Syrup**

2 dashes Owl and Whale cherry bitters

1 maraschino cherry, as garnish

Stir over ice and pour the liquid and dirty rocks into a rocks glass. Add the garnish and guzzle.

*Nutmeg-Infused Old Overholt Rye: Crack open 10 whole nutmeg pods. Add to a 750-ml bottle of Old Overholt rye whiskey. Let infuse at least four days—nutmeg infusion happens fast—then strain and rebottle.

**Cinnamon Syrup: Combine 480 ml (2 cups) water, 400 g (2 cups) granulated sugar, and 30 g (1 oz) muddled cinnamon sticks in a saucepan. Bring to a boil and reduce to simmer for ten minutes. Cool, strain, and bottle.

gaz sez: *I don't care what time of year it is. I don't care if the weather outside is frightful. Fact is that this drinks is so darned good you'll find it real hard to stop at just one. As I learned recently . . .*

Old Man & The Sea

Andrew Winters, The Blind Rabbit, Anaheim, CA, USA

Andrew says: "Thank you for this opportunity."

Apple wood chips
60 ml (2 oz) Bulleit bourbon
30 ml (1 oz) Zaya rum
7.5 ml (.25 oz) Fernet Branca
7.5 ml (.25 oz) Cinnamon Simple Syrup*
1 orange twist

Put wood chips on a fireproof plate. Create the smoke by lighting on fire and then smothering the fire by setting a room-temperature rocks glass over the chips. This can take a minute so do it first, and make sure the glass is nice and foggy before you make the cocktail.

Stir remaining ingredients over ice. Turn the rocks glass upright, letting the smoke loft out as you strain into the glass. Flame the twist over the drink, then discard.

*Cinnamon Simple Syrup: Break up 5 cinnamon sticks and add to a pot with 240 ml (1 cup) water. Bring to a boil. Immediately turn off the heat and let steep for 10 minutes. Strain the cinnamon water, return to the pot and bring back to a boil. Slowly add 400 g (2 cups) granulated sugar, stirring constantly dissolve. Remove from the heat once the sugar is completely dissolved. (Do not allow the syrup to boil for too long or it will be too thick once it cools.) Allow to cool completely for 30 minutes at room temperature before bottling. Shelf Life: 2 weeks

gaz sez: *Rum, Bourbon, Fernet, Cinnamon Simple? Of course it works. Anyone can see that. The smoked glass, though, is what helps this baby stand head and shoulders above the rest of the Chorus Line. Nice touch, Andrew.*

Once Upon A Thyme

Alan Moore, Upstairs @ KinaraKitchen, Dublin, Ireland

Alan says: "This is a cocktail I created for the Written Word phase of Diageo World Class 2015. The project was to take two books, one a cocktail book the other a novel. The two books I chose for this were Harry's ABC of Mixing Cocktails from Harry's Bar in Paris and the novel being one of my favorites, The Count of Monte Cristo. I chose the books because they fitted perfectly with each other and with what I was thinking of. Harry's book because of Edmond being arrested before he got his chance to deliver his letter to Paris. That is the theme I went with. I chose a Gimlet as the base of the cocktail because

Edmond was a sailor, next I used the thyme liqueur to represent the time Edmond spent in prison. The lavender syrup represents the area of Marseilles. The Aphrodite bitters represents his love for Mercedes and eventually Haydee. The Tincture represents the time it took him to exact his revenge on those who did him wrong. The soda (which I actually left out in the competition—I carbonated the drink in a soda siphon because I was over on the amount of ingredients) adds a slight carbonation to the drink, giving it a lovely refreshing taste, something which on a warm summer's day is great."

15 ml (.5 oz) fresh lime juice

2 barspoons caster sugar (superfine)

30 ml (1 oz) Tanqueray No. TEN gin

15 ml (.5 oz) Farigoule thyme liqueur

10 ml (.33 oz) lavender syrup (I use Monin)

2 dashes Thyme Tincture*

1 dash Dr. Adam Elmegirab's Aphrodite bitters

Soda

1 lime twist

1 thyme sprig, as garnish

Stir the lime juice and sugar in a mixing glass to dissolve the sugar. Add the gin, liqueur, syrup, tincture, and bitters. Shake over ice and double-strain into a chilled Nick & Nora glass. Top with soda. Squeeze the twist over the drink and discard, then add the garnish.

*Thyme Tincture: Infuse 500 ml (17 oz) of neutral spirit with 40 to 50 sprigs of fresh thyme for 2 weeks. Strain through a double layer of dampened cheesecloth and store in a bottle.

gaz sez: *Once upon a time I tasted a cocktail that was incredibly well balanced, multidimensional, and absolutely delicious. That was Once Upon A Thyme.*

Peace Offering

Josh Powell, 68 and Boston, London, UK

Josh says: "I created this twist for the menu in this new venue in London. It's a twist on a Paloma. Our bar takes a large influence in wines from around the world, and my menu here reflects this. This is one of my favourite serves."

25 ml (.8 oz) Olmeca reposado tequila
25 ml (.8 oz) Cocchi Vermouth di Torino
20 ml (.66 oz) Argentinian Malbec
5 ml (.16 oz or 1 teaspoon) agave syrup
Grapefruit soda
1 grapefruit twist, as garnish
Freeze 100 ml (3.4 oz) of water in a simple glass decanter.
Shake ingredients over ice and fine-strain into the decanter. Top up to the neck with soda. Add the garnish and serve with a straw.

gaz sez: *This is one of my fave serves, too. Don't it look so elegant in that bottle? The flavors, too, are pretty suave, and the Malbec is an unusual ingredient to use in a tequila drink, but it works amazingly well.*

Picasso Sour

Sean Halse, GOLD ON 26, Dubai, UAE

Sean says: "I wanted the drink to represent the artistic side of the modern bartender and used Picasso as my muse. Picasso also being famous for being a big absinthe drinker made the whole concept work, which is why I garnished with 'The Absinthe Drinker' painting by him. The signature stencil on top represents Picasso signing his bills with his signature as he started to get famous."

40 ml (1.35 oz) Kappa pisco

15 ml (.5 oz) orange curaçao

30 ml (1 oz) fresh lemon juice

20 ml (.66 oz) egg white

10 ml (.33 oz) sugar

3 dashes Absinthe

Angostura bitters, as garnish

Dry-shake, then add ice and shake again. Strain into a chilled coupe. Use a stencil, if you like, to add the garnish.

gaz sez: *I really really really love this drink. The balance is pretty incredible, the simplicity puts it into a classic category, and oh, it's a very moor-ish potion.*

Pilgrim Cocktail

*Original recipe by Dale DeGroff (created at the Rainbow Room, NY, in 1995), from *The Craft of the Cocktail* (Clarkson Potter, 2002)

Jill DeGroff says: "Back when Dale was working the Rainbow Room, he became friends with the photo editors from the Associated Press—who made a habit of taking their lunch break at his bar—naturally they loved his drinks. One Thanksgiving, Dale decided to surprise them by creating a holiday cocktail especially for them: The Pilgrim's Cocktail.

"It was a bitter cold day so he heated it the drink and poured into an insulated coffee pot on a silver tray with twelve stemmed crystal glasses. With tray in hand, dressed in his red Rainbow Room jacket, he rode down the elevator, fought his way through the holiday throngs gathered in Rockefeller Plaza, wove his way across the street to the Associated Press building, grabbed an elevator to the fourth floor, and personally delivered twelve Pilgrim Cocktails to a very happy holiday staff. Now that's what you call service!"

15 ml (.5 oz) dark rum
15 ml (.5 oz) light rum
15 ml (.5 oz) orange curaçao
60 ml (2 oz) fresh orange juice
15 ml (.5 oz) fresh lime juice
7.5 ml (.25 oz) St. Elizabeth Allspice Dram
1 dash Dale DeGroff's Pimento Aromatic bitters

Shake and strain into a cocktail glass.
Can be served hot or cold.

gaz sez: *I found this recipe on Facebook, and although the drink isn't "new" per se, it's a damned good quaff and it carries with it a pretty fabulous story that gives us a glimpse at Dale and who he was before he became King Cocktail. What he did with this drink is the stuff legends are made from, and Dale, beyond a shadow of a doubt, is a man who is far, far better than his legend. You see me, you ask me, I got Dale stories that will make you smile very large, indeed.*

Pine-y the Elder

Andrew Aoun, TAPS Fish House & Brewery, Brea, CA, USA

Andrew says: "A riff on the Russian River Brewing Company's Pliny the Elder IPA. Citrusy, refreshing, and crisp."

30 ml (1 oz) Sipsmith gin

30 ml (1 oz) Amaro Braulio

22.5 ml (.75 oz) fresh lemon juice

22.5 ml (.75 oz) rich simple syrup (2:1)

Soda water

IPA

1 lemon twist, as garnish

1 miniature pinecone, as garnish

Shake over ice and strain into a chilled collins glass. Add ice and top with a splash of soda and IPA. Stir briefly to incorporate. Form the lemon twist into a rose and add the garnishes.

gaz sez: *I had to try this just so I could try Braulio amaro (which is pretty gorgeous), and of course it also gave me a chance to drink more Sipsmith gin, an opportunity that I'd never pass up. It's a tough life I have. This whole thing comes together really well—it's refreshing, tart, and it packs a nice wallop.*

Pirate Hook

Justin Southam, ReviveR, Gosford, New South Wales, Australia

Justin says: "This drink is the end result of a lot of experiments inspired by the Meat Hook and Vieux Carre. After much deliberation, one night whilst making a "surprise me" request for a regular, this was the riff on the classic that stuck. It also saw me through to the State Finals of the Suntory Cup Australia competition. The Pirate Hook, named for its predecessor, is still a menu item and a favourite of our rum and Manhattan drinkers at ReviveR."

> 45 ml (1.5 oz) Mount Gay XO rum
> 7.5 ml (.25 oz) Punt E Mes
> 7.5 ml (.25 oz) Strega
> 7.5 ml (.25 oz) Rittenhouse 100-proof Rye whiskey
> 1 flamed orange twist, as garnish
> Stir the first three ingredients over ice and strain into chilled coupette. Then float the rye and add the garnish.

gaz sez: *The Punt E Mes and the Strega thrust and parry in this drink, and neither one of them manages to overcome the other. Instead, they come together in harmony providing a glorious backdrop to the Mount Gay XO, the lead role here. And I do love that Justin pours the Rittenhouse Rye down a sword when he floats it atop the drink! Avast, there, Matey!"*

THE RECIPES

Professor

Boudewijn Mesritz, Tales & Spirits, Amsterdam, Netherlands

"Boudewijn says: A cheeky nod to Jerry Thomas, the original professor of the cocktail world. Inspired by 4 individuals in today's cocktail industry who are forging ahead and becoming the "professors" of our era. Featuring Vermouth del Professore, Sipsmith gin, Pekoe Supreme Ceylon tea liqueur and Dr. Adam Elmegirab's Orinoco bitters. Here's to you Leonardo, Jared, Robert, & Adam! Stirred, slightly crazy and full of life! Created for the launch of the Pekoe tea liqueur and a house special at T&S! Cheers!"

40 ml (1.35 oz) Vermouth del Professore Bianco
20 ml (.66 oz) Sipsmith gin
20 ml (.66 oz) Pekoe Supreme Ceylon tea liqueur
2 dashes Dr. Adam Elmegirab's Orinoco bitters
1 grapefruit twist, as garnish
Stir over ice in a double old-fashioned glass, and add the garnish.

gaz sez: *Inspired is the first word that springs to mind when I taste this one. The Sipsmith gin delivers a sturdy backbone and great complexity, and none of the other ingredients try to fight it. The drink is in complete harmony.*

Ready, Steady, Fire!

Ralf Hubbers, Demain, Nijmegen, Gelderland, Netherlands

Ralf says: "Created for the not so honourable Dutch pirates, shooting their way through everyone and anyone, just to loot, drink and conquer the world. This drink is the aftermath, smoke rises and the ones still standing raise their glass or tankard to honour their fallen brothers."

2 to 3 pods black cardamom
40 ml (1.35 oz) Bols Genever
10 ml (.33 oz) Ilegal Mezcal Reposado
10 ml (.33 oz) yellow Chartreuse
30 ml (1 oz) fresh lime juice
20 ml (.66 oz) runny honey
2 to 3 mint sprigs, as garnish
1 to 2 grinds black pepper, as garnish

Crack the cardamom in the base of the shaker. Add ice and the remaining ingredients. Shake and fine-strain into an old-fashioned glass. Add ice and the garnishes.

gaz sez: *This drink celebrates the Dutch pirates who fought my ancestors during the spice wars, and it's hard to forgive their swashbuckling treachery even though a few hundred years have passed. Nevertheless, a damned good drink is a damned good drink no matter how you cut it, and Ready, Steady, Fire! is, for sure, a damned good drink. Nicely done, Ralf!*

Rizal

Jo-Jo Valenzuela, Brine, Fairfax, VA, USA

Jo-Jo says: "Since 2008, 50 of the best bartenders in Washington, DC compete for the title DC Craft Bartenders Guild Rickey Champion, to honor the city's official cocktail. I have submitted an entry each of the past five years, and last year I actually reached the finals but fell flat in the end. I was so bummed, because I gave my everything to that cocktail, and never thought I would be able to make anything better. On top of that, I was also voted to be the Vice President of the guild, meaning I may not be permitted to join.

"Early this year, I became an American citizen, and one thing the judge told me was my loyalty now belongs to America but to never give up my affection to my home country, the Philippines. I vowed the next time I compete, I will be using flavors I grew up with. Preparing for a different competition, I came up with flavors I miss, that grew in my home backyard, guava and kalamansi. It immediately dawned on me that I should make a soda, and ask to join the Rickey competition again which was 2 months away; I totally lost focus on the current competition.

"I called the president and the event organizer of the guild, and told them I have my made the best soda I could ever come up with, and asked them if I could compete this year. At that time the submissions were at an all-time low, so they permitted me to join as long as I do not expect to be one of the judges.

"I came up with my Rickey version, Rizal, named after the national hero of the Philippines. It had gin, lime, and my guavamansi soda, which had guava, kalamansi, Thai chili, lemongrass and water that I carbonated in a soda siphon. I told the judges that the (Thai) basil garnish is unnecessary, since classic Rickeys are not garnished with anything but the lime shell, but I wanted to let them experience what it smelled like in my backyard.

"Out of 48 contestants, in front of my family and the hundreds of people at the competition, after five years of wanting it, I cried as I got crowned the 2015 DC Craft Bartenders Guild Rickey Champion."

1 lime, cut in half

45 ml (1.5 oz) gin

Guavamansi Soda*

1 sprig Thai basil, as garnish

Squeeze the juice of one lime half into a highball glass and drop the lime shell into the glass. Add gin and fill halfway with guavamansi soda. Fill glass with ice. Slap the basil sprig and add it and the remaining lime half as garnish.

*Guavamansi Soda: First, make spiced syrup by combining 1600 g (3.5 lb) sugar and 1 L (1 qt) hot water in a saucepan. Bring to a boil, stirring continuously. Remove from the heat and transfer to a 4-quart cambro. Add 66 g (about 2 cups) bruised, minced lemongrass, the grated zest of 2 lemons, and 16 to 20 pieces of dried Thai chili. Cover and let cool to room temperature. Makes about 2 L (2 qt).

Mix 540 ml (18 oz) guava puree, 180 ml (6 oz) kalamansi juice, 420 ml (14 oz) Spiced Syrup, 20 g (4 teaspoons) citric acid, 1 g (.25 teaspoon) champagne yeast, and 2.6 L (90 oz or 11.25 c) filtered water in a gallon container and stir well. Divide among 12-ounce sterilized plastic bottles, cover, and let ferment at room temperature for 2 to 3 days, until the bottle hardens due to the carbonation. Refrigerate for 2 days to stop fermentation, and then it is ready to serve. Alternatively, you can omit the champagne yeast and carbonate with a soda siphon. Makes about 4 L (4 qt).

gaz sez: *Luckily for me, Jo-Jo sent me a sample of his soda, so I didn't have to brew up a batch of my own—the soda is fabulous, and I love the simplicity of this baby. Well done, Jo-Jo!*

Seventh Art

Andrew Bennett, The Classroom, Perth, Australia

Andrew says: "The drink is inspired by my love of cinema and how a great movie experience can be a work of art. The drink is built on the DNA of a sour, but aims to fast-track the experience of fat-washing. Here the umami flavours of butter and salt are leached from the popcorn instantaneously and experienced in cocktail form."

1 handful buttered popcorn
50 ml (1.7 oz) Bacardi Superior rum
10 ml (.33 oz) yellow Chartreuse
20 ml (.66 oz) fresh lemon juice
15 ml (.5 oz) simple syrup (1:1)
1 lemon twist, as garnish

Lightly muddle the popcorn in the bottom of a shaker. Add ice and the remaining ingredients. Shake hard and double-strain into a chilled coupe. Add the garnish.

gaz sez: *Muddled, buttered popcorn, indeed. How very dare he? Well, it turns out that Andrew Bennett is a brave soul, and his lack of fear benefits us all—this is a fabulous drink!*

THE RECIPES

205

Spanish Leather

Courtney Randall, Vito's, Seattle, WA, USA

Courtney says: "I came up with this drink while considering how Ancho Reyes would play off of gin. The brandy helps smooth out the rougher edges and plays nicely with the sherry."

45 ml (1.5 oz) Hayman's Old Tom gin
15 ml (.5 oz) Lustau Spanish brandy
15 ml (.5 oz) Ancho Reyes
22.5 ml (.75 oz) Lustau amontillado sherry
1 lemon twist, as garnish
Stir over ice and strain into a chilled cocktail glass. Add the garnish.

gaz sez: *Okay guys, listen up, this is a fabulous example of original thinking. Old Tom—and a damned fine Old Tom at that—brandy, sherry, and an ancho chile liqueur. Who in tarnation would think to put these ingredients together? Courtney Randall would. That's who. And it's a damned fine thing, too. Spanish leather will have a spot in my recipe book any old day.*

Stepford Sister

Jon Hughes, Bramble Bar & Lounge, Edinburgh, UK

Jon says: "For a long time, I'd wanted to create something zippy and refreshing for that perfect afternoon aperitivo moment and also to work in that old tradition of-equal-parts recipes that gave us drinks like the Twentieth Century and the Corpse Reviver #2."

20 ml (.66 oz) Beefeater gin
20 ml (.66 oz) St. Germain
20 ml (.66 oz) Amaro Nonino
20 ml (.66 oz) fresh lemon juice
5 ml (.16 oz or 1 teaspoon) sugar syrup
1 orange twist, as garnish

Shake over ice and fine-strain into a chilled coupette. Add the garnish.

gaz sez: *This baby cries when she hits the back of your throat, and she fair wails when she hits the tummy. What's she crying about: She's seldom witnessed such a fine balance in a cocktail before. Lots of thought went into this one.*

Sunset Strip

Eric Tecosky, Jones Hollywood, Los Angeles, CA, USA

37.5 ml (1.25 oz) Jack Daniel's Single Barrel whiskey

30 ml (1 oz) Aperol

30 ml (1 oz) Giffard Pamplemousse Rose

1 grapefruit twist, as garnish

Stir over ice and strain into an old-fashioned glass over fresh ice. Add the garnish.

gaz sez: *I'm on record as not having much time for Jack Daniel's Single Barrel whiskey, though Jack Black is one of my go-to whiskeys when I'm on the road. This drink fair turned my head around on the whiskey front, and it showed a unique approach when it comes to mixing with Tennessee whiskey—a tough ingredient to work with as far as I'm concerned, I think. Eric's onto something here. I'll have 77 of these, please.*

Tiffin Punch

Wasantha Wikramasinghe, cellar 59, ART Rotana hotel, Amwaj Island, Bahrain

Wasantha says: "The Tiffin Box can trace its roots back to 1811 in India. Whether it be the thousands of "tiffin-wallahs" distributing these amazing delicacies or a caring mother packing these for her children's lunch, they are now an essential part of everyday life in India. This same idea can be used here, and we aim to provide good quality tiffins at an affordable price."

45 ml (1.5 oz) Tanqueray No. TEN gin

10 ml (.33 oz) fresh lemon juice

60 ml (2 oz) fresh grapefruit juice

60 ml (2 oz) lychee juice

4 pieces fresh ginger

90 ml (3 oz) Borgo Santo prosecco

1 marinated grapefruit slice, as garnish

1 slice fresh ginger, as garnish

Prepare a Tiffin Box by adding ice to chill it, then discard and add fresh ice.

Shake the gin, juices, and ginger over ice and strain into the Tiffin Box. Pour in the prosecco, then add the garnishes.

gaz sez: *Here's a great drink served in a unique way. I gave many points to this drink because of the presentation, but the bonus is that it tastes pretty fabulous, too. Well done, Wasantha Wikramasinghe!*

Two World Hero

Kellie Thorn, Empire State South, Atlanta, GA, USA

"Kellie says: This is a pretty obvious riff of a Vieux Carré, one of my favorite classics. It's named for Marquis de Lafayette who was a "two world hero" fighting for both the American and French revolutions. A nod to the use of both French and American ingredients and the inclusion of a tea element which works very well here, but also references the Boston Tea Party."

30 ml (1 oz) Black Tea-Infused Pierre Ferrand 1840 Cognac*

22.5 ml (.75 oz) rye whiskey (Kellie recommends a bottled-in-bond or other full flavored rye)

22.5 ml (.75 oz) Cocchi Vermouth di Torino

7.5 ml (.25 oz) Red Wine Syrup**

1 dash Angostura bitters

1 mint sprig, as garnish

Stir over ice and strain into a chilled double old-fashioned glass over one block cube. Add the garnish.

*Black Tea-Infused Pierre Ferrand 1840 Cognac: Infuse 25 grams (1 scant oz) of organic black tea in a 750-ml bottle of Pierre Ferrand 1840 cognac for 10 minutes, then strain.

**Red Wine Syrup: Dissolve 200 g (1 cup) of granulated sugar in 240 ml (1 cup) of a robust red wine (we use a quality Malbec). Do not heat the red wine, as it will give cooked flavors that are undesirable.

gaz sez: *The Vieux Carré is one of my favorite tipples, too, so it's no wonder that this recipe caught my eye. I used Redemption Rye when I tested this baby, and the whole thing came together beautifully, with the tea-infused Pierre Ferrand cognac staunchly leading the way, but she allows all of her partners in this drink have their day in the sunshine, too. I think I might try just one more, please . . .*

Ultima Palabra

Simone De Luca, The Walrus Room, London, UK

Simone says: "Cocktail created for the first time at High Road House club in Chiswick, London. I used it for every other menu I created until now. A simple twist on a Last Word cocktail, the name is translated in Spanish, hence the main spirit used. Subtle smokiness, herbaceous flavour and nuttiness, with a touch of fruity and citrusy components, this cocktail hits all the spots for taste buds!"

25 ml (.8 oz) mezcal
25 ml (.8 oz) green Chartreuse
25 ml (.8 oz) maraschino liqueur
25 ml (.8 oz) pineapple juice
25 ml (.8 oz) fresh lime juice
1 thyme sprig, as garnish

Shake hard over ice (a little longer than usual to get proper dilution, otherwise flavours may be a bit too strong). Double-strain into a chilled coupette and add the garnish.

gaz sez: *I used Vida mezcal to test this baby, and it made her purr like a snow leopard. The Last Word is such a fine template for variation, and Simone pulled this one off in high style.*

Voodoo Vie

Bystrik Uko, Oblix Bar, London, UK

Bystrik says: "Another interpretation of a world famous cocktail, the Mai Tai. If you are looking for a new mystic rum classic cocktail, definitely you should try this. And the Banana and Cinnamon Shrub is so easy!"

60 ml (2 oz) Zacapa 23 rum
20 ml (.66 oz) Monin caramel syrup
20 ml (.66 oz) Banana and Cinnamon Shrub*
15 ml (.5 oz) fresh lime juice
3 dashes walnut bitters
2 to 3 mint leaves, as garnish
2 to 3 caramel sticks, as garnish

Shake well over ice and strain into an ice-filled ceramic cup. Add the garnishes.

*Banana and Cinnamon Shrub: Combine 900 g (2 lb) chopped bananas, 600 g (2 cups) caster or superfine sugar, 600 ml (2.5 cups) water, and 3 cinnamon sticks in a saucepan. Bring to a boil over medium-high heat, then reduce the heat and simmer for 20 minutes. Strain through a sieve and let cool, then add 350 ml red wine vinegar. Bottle and store in the refrigerator.

gaz sez: *Mai Tai, Your Tai, Her Tai, More Tai. However you pour it, the Mai Tai spurs creativity all over the world, and if that's what rocked Bystrik Uko's boat when he came up with this one, his vessel didn't sink—it sailed off into the sunset with a big grin on its bow. And his Banana and Cinnamon Shrub is just fabulous—don't miss it.*

Walkers N' Bitter

Ryan Haile, Parlour, Oakland, CA, USA

Ryan says: "Salt and vinegar chips, they have been my favorite since I can remember. British friend of mine would share her homeland's flavors of Branston pickle, or PG Tips, and the occasional crisps of many types. There has been an explosion of variations on this classic duo of savory and tangy, but nothing beats the good ol' salt and vinegar combo. Now, I can't say I have ever been to England, or Europe in general for that matter, and it is on my list of things to do in my life, but I can appreciate the combination of Walkers S and V crisps and a pint of bitter, in this case blending the best of three worlds and getting the thought of crisps while the bitter beer, and citrusy, juniper, gin do their job."

Salt and Malt Rim*
60 ml (2 oz) St. George Dry Rye gin
15 ml (.5 oz) IPA Syrup**
15 ml (.5 oz) fresh lemon juice
7.5 ml (.25 oz) Gran Classico Bitter
Float of IPA
1 lemon twist or hops bud, as garnish
Rim a double old-fashioned glass with the salt and malt mixture.
Shake over ice and fine-strain over fresh ice into the glass. Top with IPA and add the garnish.
*Salt and Malt Rim: Mix 1 tablespoon kosher salt with 2 teaspoons powdered malt vinegar in a shallow dish.

**IPA Syrup: Combine equal parts IPA and granulated sugar in a saucepan. Bring to a simmer, remove from heat, stir, let cool, and bottle.

gaz sez: *I'm a big lover of salt and vinegar crisps, too, so this one caught my eye very quickly. This is a weird bird, indeed, but it works very well, and I love the creativity that went into this one. Nice one, Ryan!*

We Don't Negotiate With Pirates

Joe Wild, 81 Liverpool Trading Docks, Liverpool, Merseyside, UK

Joe says: "Truffle and the spice of the falernum work really well with the Jameson's, making for a spicy, Moorish, and delicate flip."

45 ml (1.5 oz) Jameson Black Barrel Irish whiskey
15 ml (.5 oz) The Bitter Truth golden falernum
15 ml (.5 oz) Orange Blossom Truffle Honey*
1 egg
1 dash plum bitters
1 dash peach bitters
Grated tonka bean, as garnish

Dry shake, then add cubed ice and the remaining ingredients and shake again. Fine-strain into a chilled coupette. Add the garnish.

*Orange Blossom Truffle Honey: Combine 3 parts orange blossom honey, 1 part truffle honey, and 1 part water.

gaz sez: *This is the second recipe I've selected this week that calls for an Irish whiskey base. If this is the start of a trend I see some great new drinks in our future. Merseyside gave us the Beatles, and now we have Joe Wild, too. Whatever's coming from Liverpool next? Nice one, Joe!*

White Sazerac

Maroš Dzurus, HIMKOK, Oslo, Norway

Maroš says: "The Sazerac as always evolved through its history. Starting with cognac and Peychaud's bitters, then moving to rye whiskey with the addition of Absinthe.

"This is my new interpretation of this cocktail—a nice, delicate yet powerful Sazerac. It's more of a Nordic style with aquavit, Becherovka, Frangelico, simple syrup and Absinthe.

"The aquavit we produce at Himkok get very fresh notes and delicate spices, but you can use any kind of unaged aquavit. Becherovka will bring some winter flavors, replace the bitterness of the Peychaud's bitters and enhance the flavor and spices of the aquavit. Frangelico opens up the nutty taste. The spray of Absinthe and lemon are for the freshness in the drink."

Absinthe, as rinse
40 ml (1.35 oz) white aquavit
10 ml (.33 oz) Becherovka
10 ml (.33 oz) Frangelico
2.5 ml simple syrup
1 lemon twist, as garnish
Coat a coupette with Absinthe. Stir the remaining ingredients over ice and strain into the glass. Add the garnish.

gaz sez: *Himkok seems to be putting out some pretty fabulous drinks (see, also, the Bee Negroni), and this one will likely blow your socks off. Maroš sent me a small bottle of aquavit, fashioned by the one* *and only Monica Berg, in order that I could test this baby in its natural state. What can I say? Monica would never steer anyone wrong. And Maroš' recipe is to die for. Get yourself to Oslo if you must, but don't miss this one.*

White Walker

Sky Huo, Earl's Juke Joint, Sydney, NSW, Australia

Sky says: "Basically, it's a white tequila Martinez. Dolin Blanc works as a connection of blanco tequila and maraschino liqueur. This drink is simple and easy to make. But different variations of tequila or mezcal could be used."

> 45 ml (1.5 oz) Don Julio blanco tequila
> 20 ml (.66 oz) Dolin blanc vermouth
> 10 ml (.33 oz) Luxardo maraschino liqueur
> 1 dash Fee Brothers lemon bitters
> 1 lemon twist, as garnish
> Stir over ice and strain into a chilled Nick & Nora glass. Add the garnish.

gaz sez: *My dreams are coming true this year inasmuch as many very accomplished bartenders seem to be sending relatively uncomplicated cocktail recipes to me, and this is a sign, I think, that the tides are turning back to simplicity—it's a trend that I really like.*

That said, I also encourage bartenders to keep pushing the envelope, and using their creativity to the max—without the innovators, we might stagnate a little, and that would never do.

This drink works absolutely perfectly, and Sky, who I met a few years ago, really knows her craft inside out. I'm so happy to include her recipe here this year.

THE RECIPES

Wild Rover

Jimmy Hillegas, Frolik Kitchen + Cocktails, Seattle, WA, USA

Jimmy says: "To engage all senses, I have used black walnut bitters to give a sweet nutty flavor to enhance the Irish whiskey in all of its glory. Bringing a rich flavor to an already rich whiskey, adding a mint garnish with a slap to release the oils for a fragrance that hits a note with the rear tastebuds and the sweetness of bitters sugar and mild component of Jameson in the tastebuds in the front. Completing it with a dwelling background of citrus from a lemon wedge unsqueezed remaining in the beverage until completion. Stimulating 3 senses of sight, smell, and taste for a well rounded and highly enjoyable cocktail."

> 1 sugar cube
> 7 dashes black walnut bitters
> 60 ml (2 oz) Jameson Irish whiskey
> 1 lemon wedge, as garnish
> 2 mint sprigs, as garnish
>
> Muddle the sugar cube and bitters. Add ice. Add whiskey and stir, then add the garnishes.

gaz sez: *BARTENDERS TAKE NOTE! Can you say, "Less is More."? This recipe proves it. Bloody brilliant it is. Well done, Jimmy!*

Williams Christ Superstar

Björn Bochinski, Lux Bar, Münster, Germany

Björn says: "This is a German twist on one of my favourite drinks, the Old Cuban. The Jägermeister balances the fresh and dry notes of the drink and adds more complexity to the drink."

50 ml (1.7 oz) Williams Christ pear eau de vie

10 ml (.33 oz) Jägermeister

15 to 20 ml (.5 to .66 oz) fresh lemon juice, depending on the Riesling

20 ml (.66 oz) sugar syrup

8 to 10 mint leaves (reserve one as garnish)

Dry German sparkling Riesling wine

Shake all ingredients except the Riesling over ice. Fine-strain into a chilled coupette and top with the Riesling. Add the garnish.

gaz sez: *Simply deeeeelishush! I love how your brain works, Björn!*

Workers on the Tracks

Luke Andrews, The Whistler, Chicago, IL, USA

Luke says: "The goal with this drink was to be simple. Three ingredients. No acid. A drink I could write on a napkin and someone could make at home or ahead of time for a decanter (or flask). The balance only works with a big, rough-around-the-corners high-proof rye. Bourbon does not work at all. The layers of the drink unfold as it sits over ice. I recommend drinking it and preparing it the way you would make a Negroni in terms of dilution and chill. Keep your fingers out of this one. When riding the train in Chicago you will undoubtedly hear 'Your attention please…we are being delayed because there are WORKERS ON THE TRACKS ahead…' and that's when you reach for the tiny silver companion in your back pocket."

60 ml (2 oz) bonded or higher proof rye whiskey (Wild Turkey or Rittenhouse work great)
15 ml (.5 oz) Pierre Ferrand dry curaçao
15 ml (.5 oz) yellow Chartreuse
1 orange twist, as garnish
Stir over ice and strain into a rocks glass over a large piece of fresh ice. Add the garnish.

gaz sez: *Luke's gonna have a hard time trying to stop me from finger-stirring this baby—it's living proof that keeping it simple can lead to some very complex cocktails, and he's right in saying that you need a rye with some oomph to it to pull it off properly. Wild Turkey 101 or Rittenhouse Bonded do* *the trick well. This might not be a session drink, but I bet I can put two or three of these cocktails away pretty quickly.*

World Traveler

Frank Caiafa, Peacock Alley, Waldorf=Astoria, New York, NY, USA

Frank says: "Created for a guest's event, this intriguing tipple turned out to be an unintentional nod to the Old Bar. With its Holland Gin and French Vermouth and Italian Bitter (Fernet), along with an American rendition of an old world liqueur, a unique hybrid was found.

"Iris is a fine domestically produced liqueur with high floral notes and a hefty viscosity that stands up to the other ingredients, though the liqueur slot proved to be quite pliable and can be adjusted for personal taste. That said, the Italian Strega liqueur would probably come closest to achieving this profile if the small production Iris is difficult to procure. Its sister product, Calisaya liqueur would also work well. Chartreuse, maraschino, elderflower, and even a curacao such as Grand Marnier would all bring different elements to the table. Either way, I think that this ranks with only a scant few others that we created that take on the tone and soul of the Old Bar's offerings. If only Mr. O'Connor and Mr. Solon (among the other Old Bar bartenders) were around to tell us different."

>45 ml (1.5 oz) Bols Genever (Holland)
>22.5 ml (.75 oz) Noilly Prat extra dry vermouth (France)
>15 ml (.5 oz) Fernet Branca (Italy)
>15 ml (.5 oz) Iris liqueur (United States)
>2 dashes Regans' Orange Bitters No. 6
>1 lemon twist, as garnish

Stir over ice for 30 seconds and strain into chilled cocktail glass. Add the garnish.

gaz sez: *Oh yes, oh yes, oh yes! Frank Caiafa's drinks regularly appear in my 101 BNC lists, and deservedly so, too. And if you read his comments concerning the liqueurs in this formula, you'll see for your own self that Frank doesn't have a head on his shoulders, he has mixing glass in its stead—and it's a mixing glass that knows exactly what it's doing. Another great drink for the list, Frank!*

Yuliya Martini

Andrii Osypchuk, Blasé Dubai, Dubai, UAE

Andrii says: "My cocktail, the Yuliya Martini, is my twist on the vesper martini. Like James Bond named a cocktail after his love, Vesper Lynd, I have named my twist after the love of my life, my girlfriend Yuliya. The vesper martini was a mixture of vodka, gin and Kina Lillet. What many people do not know, is that the formula of Kina Lillet had changed over time, and the Lillet Blanc we know today doesn't taste much like its predecessor anymore. That is why I have chosen to use Cocchi Americano, which is far closer to the original recipe of Kina Lillet. And as Yuliya has always been my little peach, I thought that crème de pêche was a very suiting ingredient to give my drink a subtle sweetness and femininity. Combine this with a few dashes of absinthe, and the bold flavour of Belvedere, and you have what I believe is an evolution of a classic drink. The Yuliya Martini is extremely low in sugar, only a very small amount of crème de pêche, and garnished with a drop of eucalyptus oil, which is known for its medicinal quality. It's also a drink that is very easy to replicate, and is balanced in a way that smoothness of Belvedere is not hidden, but enhanced."

45 ml (1.5 oz) Belvedere Pure vodka
10 ml (.33 oz) Cocchi Americano
2 dashes absinthe
2.5 ml (.08 oz or .5 teaspoon) crème de pêche
1 grapefruit twist, as garnish
1 drop eucalyptus oil, as garnish

Shake hard over ice and double-strain into a chilled coupette. Add the garnish.

gaz sez: *Look here, all ye Vesper haters, and shudder. This guy knows how to fix a flawed classic, and he does it with great style. The absinthe and crème de pêche play so well together you're going to be amazed. Promise.*

www.ingramcontent.com/pod-product-compliance
Lightning Source LLC
Chambersburg PA
CBHW051606170426
43196CB00038B/2944